DISEASES AND DISORDERS

SLEEP DISORDERS

WHAT KEEPS PEOPLE UP AT NIGHT?

By Simon Pierce

Portions of this book originally appeared in *Sleep Disorders* by Barbara Sheen.

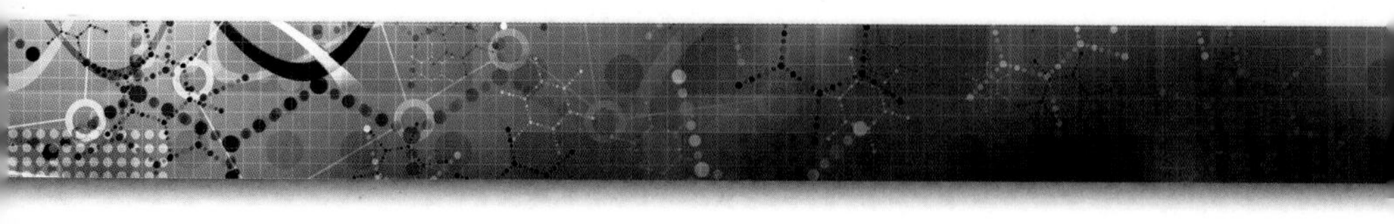

Published in 2020 by
Lucent Press, an Imprint of Greenhaven Publishing, LLC
353 3rd Avenue
Suite 255
New York, NY 10010

Designer: Deanna Paternostro
Editor: Jennifer Lombardo

Library of Congress Cataloging-in-Publication Data

Names: Pierce, Simon, author.
Title: Sleep disorders : what keeps people up at night? / Simon Pierce.
Description: New York : Lucent Press, [2020] | Series: Diseases and disorders | Includes bibliographical references and index.
Identifiers: LCCN 2018043989 (print) | LCCN 2018046006 (ebook) | ISBN 9781534567528 (eBook) | ISBN 9781534567511 (paperback book) | ISBN 9781534566927 (library bound book)
Subjects: LCSH: Sleep disorders–Diagnosis. | Sleep disorders–Treatment.
Classification: LCC RC547 (ebook) | LCC RC547 .P54 2020 (print) | DDC 616.8/498–dc23
LC record available at https://lccn.loc.gov/2018043989

Printed in the United States of America

CPSIA compliance information: Batch #BS19KL: For further information contact Greenhaven Publishing LLC, New York, New York, at 1-844-317-7404.

Please visit our website, www.greenhavenpublishing.com. For a free color catalog of all our high-quality books, call toll free 1-844-317-7404 or fax 1-844-317-7405.

CONTENTS

FOREWORD

Illness is an unfortunate part of life, and it is one that is often misunderstood. Thanks to advances in science and technology, people have been aware for many years that diseases such as the flu, pneumonia, and chickenpox are caused by viruses and bacteria. These diseases all cause physical symptoms that people can see and understand, and many people have dealt with these diseases themselves. However, sometimes diseases that were previously unknown in most of the world turn into epidemics and spread across the globe. Without an awareness of the method by which these diseases are spread—through the air, through human waste or fluids, through sexual contact, or by some other method—people cannot take the proper precautions to prevent further contamination. Panic often accompanies epidemics as a result of this lack of knowledge.

Knowledge is power in the case of mental disorders, as well. Mental disorders are just as common as physical disorders, but due to a lack of awareness among the general public, they are often stigmatized. Scientists have studied them for years and have found that they are generally caused by chemical imbalances in the brain, but they have not yet determined with certainty what causes those imbalances or how to fix them. Because even mild mental illness is stigmatized in Western society, many people prefer not to talk about it.

Chronic pain disorders are also not well understood—even by researchers—and do not yet have foolproof treatments. People who have a mental disorder or a disease or disorder that causes them to feel chronic pain can be the target of uninformed opinions. People who do not have these disorders sometimes struggle to understand how difficult it can be to deal with the symptoms. These disorders are often termed "invisible illnesses" because no one can see the symptoms; this leads many people to doubt that they exist or are serious problems. Additionally, people who have an undiagnosed disorder may understand that they are experiencing the world in a different way than their peers, but they have no one to turn to for answers.

Misinformation about all kinds of ailments is often spread through personal anecdotes, social media, and even news sources. This series aims to present accurate information about both physical and mental conditions so young adults will have a better understanding of them. Each volume discusses the symptoms of a particular disease or disorder, ways it is currently being treated, and the research that is being done to understand it further. Advice for people who may be suffering from a disorder is included, as well as information for their loved ones about how best to support them.

With fully cited quotes, a list of recommended books and websites for further research, and informational charts, this series provides young adults with a factual introduction to common illnesses. By learning more about these ailments, they will be better able to prevent the spread of contagious diseases, show compassion to people who are dealing with invisible illnesses, and take charge of their own health.

INTRODUCTION

UNDERSTANDING SLEEP DISORDERS

Nearly everyone has experienced an occasional night of sleeplessness. When the room is too hot or too cold, when a new baby is in the household and crying during the night, or when someone is especially worried about something, it can be difficult for a person to fall asleep or stay asleep. However, for some people, a medical problem prevents them from getting restful sleep nearly every night.

A sleep disorder is a condition that affects normal patterns of sleep and wakefulness. Some sleep too little, some sleep too much, and some have their sleep interrupted. Generally, the quality of their sleep is poor, so most wake up still feeling tired. As a result, their overall health, emotional well-being, and ability to function all suffer.

A Common Problem

According to the American Sleep Association, anywhere from 50 million to 70 million American adults have a sleep disorder. Additionally, a poll by a different organization—the National Sleep Foundation—found that "two out of every three children ages 10 and under have experienced some type of sleep problem."[1] Sleep disorders affect people of every age, ethnicity, and social background.

Experts say the number of sleep disorders is on the rise; about 40 percent of Americans reported sleeping for 6 hours or less per night in 2013, compared

Newborn babies frequently cry during the night, which can disrupt the sleep of the other members of the household. However, this is different than having a sleep disorder.

to 11 percent in 1942. Some people believe modern life is intensifying the problem. Some medications can cause sleep problems, and mental illnesses such as post-traumatic stress disorder (PTSD) can as well. Among U.S. veterans in particular, sleep disorder diagnosis increased from less than 1 percent to almost 6 percent in just 11 years. The rate of PTSD diagnosis among this group has also increased in that time. Additionally, the blue light that TV, phone, and computer screens give off has been found to disrupt the body's natural sleep rhythms if devices are used too close to bedtime. The rise in obesity that has taken place in recent decades has also been found to be a factor, since weight can affect sleep quality.

Many people voluntarily choose to do things that cause them to get less sleep than they need, such as staying up late to watch a movie, read a good book, or finish homework. In an article for *AARP the Magazine*, a publication aimed at people over the age of 50, journalist David Dudley mentioned "'sleep-shaming'—when alpha-achiever types humblebrag about how late they work and how early they rise."[2] This type of bragging can make other people feel as though they also have to sleep less and work more to avoid being seen as lazy. Dudley noted that sleep-shaming is not a recent occurrence, since Thomas Edison used to claim that he only needed to sleep four hours and expected his employees to do the same. The idea of sleeping as a waste of time has persisted throughout history, making people feel guilty about getting enough sleep. Many people also blame modern work and school schedules for forcing them to choose not to get enough sleep.

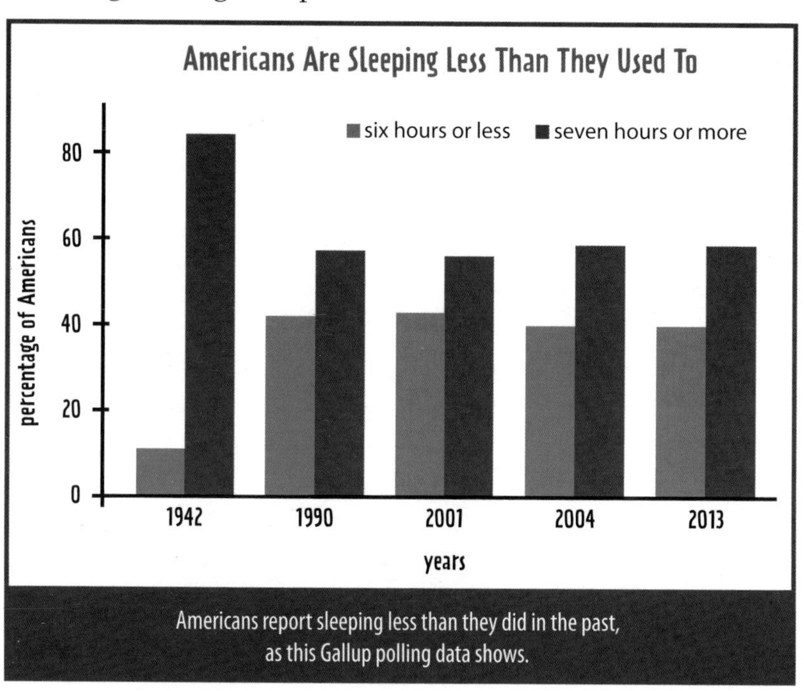

Americans report sleeping less than they did in the past, as this Gallup polling data shows.

Voluntary sleep deprivation is not a disorder, but over time it can disrupt healthy sleep rhythms, resulting in a true sleep disorder—so when these individuals want to get more sleep, they cannot. According to sleep expert Dr. Matthew Edlund,

> *People have turned themselves into machines ... They're working 24/7. But they're not machines, and their bodies aren't getting the needed rest to rebuild and renew ...*

> *More people are developing insomnia, so they use sleeping pills to sleep, then using stimulants like caffeine to stay awake. They race through the day, instead of going with the natural flow and rhythm. I'm saying they shouldn't fight the need to rest. The body needs time to rebuild.*[3]

The Problem with Sleep Disorders

Sleep disorders not only impact the individuals who suffer from them, they have a huge impact on society as a whole. This is especially true when sleep-deprived drivers get behind the wheel of a motor vehicle. When individuals do not get enough high-quality sleep, their judgment, motor skills, and alertness are impaired. They put themselves and everyone in their path at risk. The National Heart, Lung, and Blood Institute, which is a division of the National Institutes of Health (NIH), reported that "sleep deficiency harms your driving ability as much as, or more than, being drunk."[4] According to the National Highway Traffic Safety Administration, sleepy drivers caused about 72,000 crashes, 800 deaths, and 44,000 injuries in 2013. However, the Centers for Disease Control and Prevention (CDC) noted that these numbers are likely smaller than the real total because the cause of some crashes cannot be determined.

Sleep disorders also cause problems in the workplace and at school because they make it harder for people to concentrate on their work. As a result, workers may fall behind, causing stress and other issues, and students' grades may suffer. Sleep deprivation is also the cause of many workplace accidents, which can endanger the health and safety of both the sleep-deprived person and their coworkers. For example, a 2011 Harvard Medical School study examined the effect of sleep deprivation on police officers. The study screened 4,957 police officers and found that 40 percent had sleep disorders. Compared with their less-sleepy peers, sleep-deprived officers were more likely to have poorer overall health, were more likely to be injured on the job, and were more likely to lose their tempers with suspects, which resulted in more citizen complaints against them.

Being sleep-deprived can make driving extremely dangerous.

Knowledge Is Power

Clearly, sleep disorders impact everyone, but many people do not understand the importance of sleep. It is common for people to believe that they can function on little sleep better than they actually can, and some take a long time to see the pattern in their sleeplessness. Therefore, they do not discuss their sleep problems with their doctors, which means many people go undiagnosed. This is particularly troubling because sleep disorders can be treated. The best way to solve this problem is for people to learn more about sleep and sleep disorders. Armed with knowledge, they can make lifestyle changes and seek help for themselves and their loved ones.

CHAPTER ONE

HOW SLEEP WORKS

Sleep is a necessary part of life. In addition to giving people enough energy and concentration to deal with everyday activities, it plays an important role in mental and physical health. Sleep helps the body repair itself when it is injured or ill, reduces the risk of health problems such as heart attack and stroke, balances the level of hormones in the brain, and promotes healthy growth in young adults. Understanding how sleep works is the first step in understanding how sleep disorders affect people.

More to Understand

Like food, water, and oxygen, all animals need sleep to survive. There is no substitute for sleep. Humans spend approximately one-third of their lives sleeping or trying to sleep. Even minimal sleep loss impacts a person's physical, mental, and emotional health. Chronic sleep deprivation is so harmful that it has been classified as a form of torture; for this reason, in 2014, the United Nations (UN) condemned the United States for using long-term sleep deprivation on political prisoners.

However, despite the amount of time people spend sleeping, much about it is a mystery. For example, it is known that staying awake for too long can lead to psychosis and death, but no one is sure exactly how long is "too long." Some people begin to hallucinate after only 24 hours without sleep, while others can go for days before experiencing a psychotic break. Scientists are also not completely certain what, exactly, the brain does when a person is asleep or why it is so necessary for health. People also question why humans and animals evolved to need sleep. As psychology professor Christopher French pointed out in an article for *Scientific American*, "sleep appears to be incompatible with survival because it prevents feeding and procreation and could expose the sleeper to attack by predators. Sleep must confer [give] some essential benefits to outweigh these serious disadvantages."[5] One of the most popular theories is that sleep evolved to help animals save energy when food is hard to find or when they are likely to be attacked.

Sleep may be a way for animals to save energy when there is not enough food in their area.

However, one thing scientists do know is that the brain is active during sleep. Until 1953, when Dr. Nathaniel Kleitman and one of his students, Eugene Aserinsky, proved this fact, scientists believed that sleep was a passive state in which the brain shuts down. Using an electroencephalograph (EEG), a device that records brain-wave patterns, Kleitman monitored and compared the brain activity of test subjects while they were awake and while they were asleep. During an EEG, small electrodes and wires are attached to a subject's scalp. The electrodes detect electrical signals that are produced by the brain. These signals form patterns known as brain waves. The EEG machine records the brain waves as a graph on paper or on a computer screen.

Kleitman's test showed that the brain produces electrical activity during sleep as well as wakefulness. If the accepted theory that the brain shuts down during sleep were correct, then an EEG test on sleeping subjects would not have detected any activity. Although the brain-wave patterns recorded during sleep were different from those recorded during wakefulness, it was clear that the brain remained active during sleep.

Kleitman's study led to more research. Scientists now know that the brain performs a number of important jobs during sleep that are necessary to maintain good health. These include repairing, healing, and replacing damaged cells; directing the release of hormones that control growth, sexual characteristics, and appetite; restoring chemical balance; producing insulin, a hormone that regulates blood sugar; lowering blood pressure; strengthening the immune system; processing the experiences and emotions of the day; and creating and storing memories.

Stages in the Sleep Cycle

Healthy sleep is divided into cycles. Each cycle has three initial stages called non-rapid eye movement (NREM) stages. They are known as N1, N2, and N3. Previously NREM sleep was considered to have four stages, but in 2007, sleep specialists realized the last two stages were essentially the same, so they were combined as N3. NREM sleep is followed by rapid eye movement, or REM, sleep. Each stage produces different brain-wave patterns, which makes it possible to recognize the stages with an EEG. The brain typically cycles through the three initial stages and REM sleep four to five times per night. A complete cycle of NREM lasts about 90 minutes, but the amount of time individuals spend in each stage of a sleep cycle changes as the sleep period progresses. Sleep disorders can interrupt, shorten, or disrupt the order of the stages or prevent one or more stages from occurring. Healthy sleep requires all the cycles to occur in the same order over the full course of 90 minutes.

N1 serves as a transition between wakefulness and sleep, and it lasts about 5 to 10 minutes. During this stage, an individual's brain and body begin to relax and body temperature decreases. Brain waves change from a combination of beta waves (rapid brain waves that dominate during wakefulness) and alpha waves (slower brain waves that occur when people are awake and relaxed) to mainly alpha waves. Breathing becomes more regular, the eyes move slowly under the eyelids, and muscle activity decreases. People often feel as if

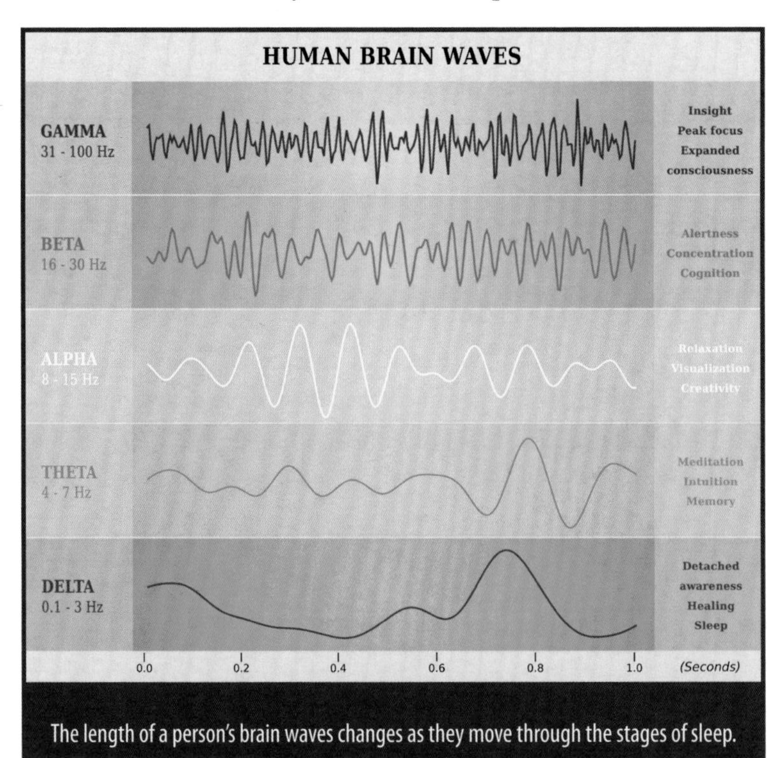

The length of a person's brain waves changes as they move through the stages of sleep.

they are floating, drifting, or falling during this time. Because N1 is a very light sleep stage, sleepers can be awakened easily, and, if they are awakened, they may think that they were not asleep at all.

The Ideal Sleep Pattern?

Many people wake up in the middle of the night and take about an hour to fall back asleep. This can be frustrating, especially when people know they have to get up in a few short hours. However, some experts say this is a natural sleep pattern called a biphasic pattern. Sleep historian Roger Ekirch explained that in the past,

> *Humans slept in two four-hour blocks, which were separated by a period of wakefulness in the middle of the night lasting an hour or more. During this time some might stay in bed, pray, think about their dreams, or talk with their spouses. Others might get up and do tasks or even visit neighbors before going back to sleep.*[1]

People slept this way, Ekirch said, because before the light bulb was invented, there could be up to 14 hours of darkness in a day. People could not stay up and do things when they could not see, so they had to go to bed, but they did not need 14 full hours of sleep. After electricity became common, the day became structured differently, with people staying up until late at night. According to Live Science, "Now, 'normal' sleep requires forgoing the periods of wakefulness that used to break up the night; we simply don't have time for a midnight chat with the neighbor any longer. 'But people with particularly strong circadian rhythms continue to [wake up in the night],' said Ekirch."[2] Studies suggest that the biphasic sleep pattern is the one humans naturally evolved to have.

1. Quoted in Natalie Wolchover, "Busting the 8-Hour Sleep Myth: Why You Should Wake Up in the Night," Live Science, February 16, 2011. www.livescience.com/12891-natural-sleep.html.

2. Wolchover, "Busting the 8-Hour Sleep Myth."

N2 is a deeper stage of sleep. It lasts about 10 to 25 minutes. During this stage, slower brain waves called theta waves are the most active. Sleepers' breathing and heartbeat slow and hold steady, their muscles relax even further, and their eye movement stops. This is still considered light sleep. People spend more time in N2 over the course of the night than in any other stage.

N3 is the deepest stage of sleep. It is also known as slow-wave sleep (SWS) because during this stage, sleepers' brain waves slow down, and delta waves, which are the slowest of all brain waves, take over. At this stage, sleepers' bodies are very relaxed, their body temperature is low, and their heartbeat and breathing are very slow and regular. It is difficult to wake a sleeper during N3. If individuals are awakened, they are generally confused and still sleepy. This is why experts recommend that people nap for no more than 30 minutes so they can avoid falling into N3. This stage lasts about 20 to 40 minutes for adults; babies and young children spend more time in N3.

Often, people with sleep disorders do not get sufficient N3 sleep because they awaken frequently during the night. This can affect their general health, since this is the stage in which the brain performs much of its repair work on the body, regulates hormones, builds up energy for the next day, and strengthens memory.

The REM Stage

After about 90 minutes, sleepers enter REM sleep. REM sleep is characterized by active eye movement, where sleepers' eyes move back and forth rapidly under closed eyelids. During REM sleep, sleepers' brain activity intensifies. Alpha and beta brain waves dominate, making the brain-wave pattern look more like that of wakefulness than of deep sleep. Sleepers' body temperature falls, but their blood pressure, heart rate, and breathing rate rise. REM sleep is also when dreaming occurs. Although sleepers' small muscles may twitch, their skeletal muscles are temporarily paralyzed. Scientists think this may be the body's way of protecting itself from physically reacting to dreams. Sleepers also dream during NREM sleep, but dreams are more concentrated in REM sleep, and REM dreams are longer and more vivid.

Why people dream or what significance dreams play is another mystery. Some sleep experts think that dreaming stimulates creativity and helps with problem solving. They think it is the brain's way of processing what happened during the day, creating memories, and working through emotional issues. Others believe dreams are just random, meaningless firings of the neurons in the brain. One 2017 study suggested that dreams reduce stress and anxiety; according to *TIME* magazine, "getting sufficient REM sleep prior to fearful experiences may make a person less prone to developing post-traumatic stress disorder (PTSD)."[6] The researchers came to this conclusion by giving mild electric shocks to study participants. Those who had gotten a lot of REM sleep the previous night showed less fear-related brain activity in response to the shocks. Scientists do know that the length of dreams varies and that when individuals are awakened from REM sleep, they generally have strong recollections of their dreams.

Dreams may be a way for people to work out their fears or desires and to process things they have encountered during the day. Often, dreams do not seem to make sense.

The exact function of REM sleep is unknown, but research suggests that it is very important, especially for mental health. *TIME* explained,

> *Several studies in recent years have suggested that REM sleep can affect how accurately people can read emotions and process external stimuli. [Psychology professor Matthew] Walker's research, for example, has demonstrated that people who achieved REM sleep during a nap were better able to judge facial expressions afterward than those who'd napped without reaching REM.*
>
> *Walker and his colleagues have also found that people who view emotional images before getting a good night's sleep are less likely to have strong reactions to the same images the next day, compared to those who didn't sleep well.*[7]

REM sleep makes up 20 to 25 percent of a person's total sleep time. When it ends, the sleep cycle begins again. As the sleep period goes on, the duration of REM sleep increases from about 10 minutes for the first episode to about 1 hour for the last. In contrast, NREM sleep decreases. N3, especially, becomes briefer and briefer toward the end of the total sleep period. Since awakening from N3 leaves individuals feeling groggy, shortening the duration of N3 near the time of awakening may be the brain's way of making sure individuals wake up feeling refreshed.

Homeostasis and Circadian Rhythms

Exactly when individuals fall asleep and when they wake up is controlled by two important mechanisms called homeostasis and circadian rhythms. Homeostasis keeps the body in balance so it can function correctly. Among other things, homeostasis drives the body to sleep when it is tired.

Dream Interpretation

For centuries, people have believed that the things they dream about have symbolic meanings. For example, some people believe dreams where someone is being chased may indicate that a person is running away from an uncomfortable situation and dreams of a person's teeth falling out may represent that the dreamer feels out of control. Some people even believe dreams can predict the future.

Sometimes a person can clearly identify where an element of their dream is coming from. For example, someone who watches a horror movie right before bed may have a nightmare about the movie. Other times, dream elements seem completely disconnected from a person's life. Dream interpretation can be fun and is a harmless activity, but many researchers believe there is no scientific basis to it.

The brain also regulates the body's circadian rhythm, its daily internal clock, which works with homeostasis and with the external environment to coordinate sleep and wakefulness. The body's circadian clock is like an alarm clock in the brain that is controlled by light and darkness. Darkness signals the clock that it is time to sleep, which causes the brain to release melatonin, a chemical that makes people feel sleepy. Light coming in through the eyelids suppresses the release of melatonin and signals the clock that it is time to wake up. In some sleep disorders, the circadian clock may be disturbed, delaying the release of melatonin. The release of melatonin can also be disrupted if individuals are deprived of sunlight during the day or exposed to excessive light at night. Recent studies have found that the blue light that comes from TV, phone, or computer screens can affect the body's melatonin production, causing changes in the circadian rhythm. This causes people to take longer to fall asleep, get less REM sleep, and take longer to wake up. For this reason, several apps have been developed to add a red filter to screens in the evening, which makes the blue light less intense. However, experts recommend that for the best sleep, people should avoid using their devices completely at least 1 hour before bed.

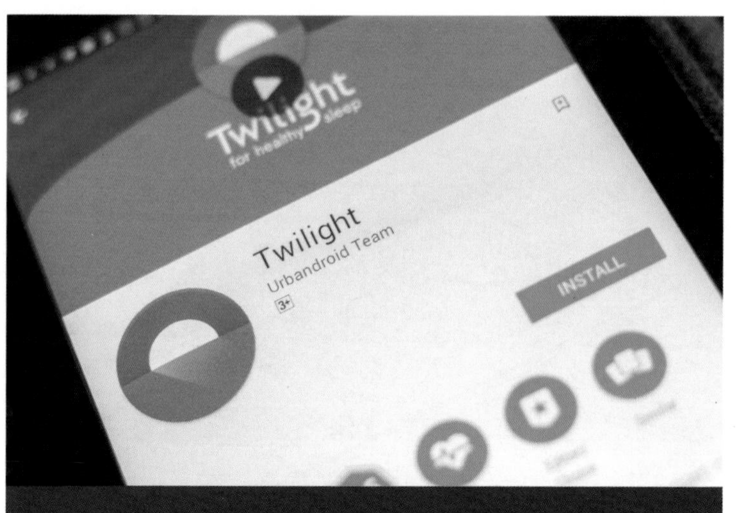

Apps such as f.lux and Twilight have been developed to make screens look more red at night, decreasing the amount of blue light a person's eyes are absorbing near bedtime.

Unfortunately, for some people, this is difficult to do. Modern work and school schedules sometimes make it necessary for people to stay up late completing homework and other tasks. The typical school schedule, in particular, has been criticized as a major cause of sleeplessness in young adults. Experts say teens need between 9 and 10 hours of sleep per night but generally only get about 7. According to Nationwide Children's Hospital, "Some high schools start as early as 7:00 AM, meaning that some teenagers have to get up as early as 5:00 AM to get ready for and travel to school."[8] Added to this is the fact that many students are assigned several hours of homework each night. Balancing this workload as well as extracurricular activities and time with friends leaves little time for sleep. For this reason, the American Academy of Pediatrics (AAP) issued a statement in 2014 recommending that schools start no earlier than 8:30 a.m.

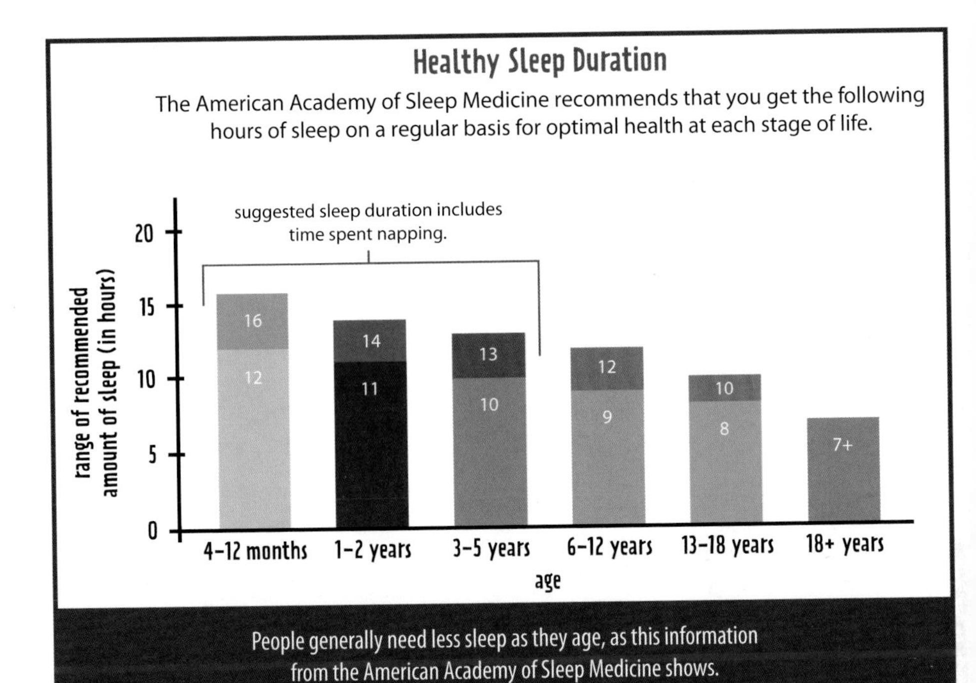

People generally need less sleep as they age, as this information from the American Academy of Sleep Medicine shows.

The Right Amount of Sleep

Not everyone needs the same amount of sleep. The amount of sleep people require depends on a number of factors. Age is one of the most important. On average, adults need about 8 hours of sleep per night to maintain good health. Teenagers need at least 9 hours. Children between the ages of 5 and 12 need 9 to 10 hours, children under 5 need 11 to 13 hours, and infants need about 16 hours.

The amount of sleep individuals need increases if they are sick, elderly, pregnant, or did not get enough sleep the night before. Sleep debt is the term given to the difference between the amount of sleep individuals need and the amount of sleep they get. Every time people sleep less than they should, they add to their sleep debt. People with sleep disorders generally have very large sleep debts.

Like financial debt, sleep debt should be paid back. Many people try to pay back their sleep debt by sleeping longer on the weekend or on their days off from work or school. However, a few hours of extra sleep on Saturday cannot pay back the sleep debt of individuals who are chronically sleep deprived. In fact, sleep experts say that altering the sleep schedule on weekends can throw off a person's circadian rhythm, making it harder for them to fall asleep during the week.

According to Sleep.org, a website run by the National Sleep Foundation, "when you're in the grips of sleep debt, you often don't even remember what

Stages of Sleep Deprivation

Everyone's body reacts slightly differently to not getting enough sleep. However, in general, there are several noticeable effects that come with not getting any sleep at all for long periods of time.

- At 24 hours, a person's judgment, thought process, and reaction time is impaired. A study published in the *International Journal of Occupational Medicine and Environmental Health* found that the effects of going without sleep for 24 hours are similar to having a blood alcohol content (BAC) of 0.10 percent. According to clinical sleep educator Terry Cralle, "You're more emotional, attention is decreased, hearing is impaired, and there is an increase in your risk of death from a fatal accident."[1]
- At 36 hours, a person's health starts noticeably suffering. They may feel faint, have difficulty remembering what has happened in the last few minutes or hours, and lose motivation to perform tasks. They are also even more emotional than they were at 24 hours of sleep deprivation.
- At 48 hours, the person begins experiencing microsleeps, which is when the body falls asleep for half a second to half a minute. The person does not realize what has happened but is generally disoriented when they come back to consciousness. Microsleeps can be dangerous if the person is doing something such as driving or operating a machine at the time.
- At 72 hours, the person begins to hallucinate and experiences "significant deficits in concentration, motivation, perception, and other higher mental processes."[2]

1. Quoted in Mikel Theobald, "What Happens to You When You Don't Sleep for Days," Everyday Health, last updated January 31, 2018. www.everydayhealth.com/conditions/what-happens-when-you-dont-sleep-days/.

2. Theobald, "What Happens to You When You Don't Sleep for Days."

it's like to feel well rested, so you may not realize just how tired you are."[9] Eventually, however, the brain will insist that sleep debt be paid off. Coming down with a cold or flu, which causes someone to stay in bed and sleep, is one way the body may try to catch up. To avoid this, people can make certain changes to their routine to slowly pay back their sleep debt by getting an extra hour or two of sleep per night. These include going to bed earlier, waking up at the same time each day, avoiding long naps, and identifying lifestyle changes that can make sticking to a sleep schedule easier. Someone with a sleep disorder generally needs to make additional changes, such as taking medication.

How Sleep Debt Affects the Body

Even a small sleep debt can affect a person's health. For people with sleep disorders who have large sleep debts, the effects on the body can be overwhelming. Sleep deprivation has been linked to heart disease, high blood pressure, obesity, diabetes, headaches, backaches, general pain, memory loss, and shortened attention span. A 2008 University of Chicago study found that lack of sleep increases the buildup of plaque, a form of hardened fats, calcium, and other material in the arteries. Plaque is dangerous because it can break off and block smaller blood vessels, causing a heart attack or stroke. The researchers looked at 495 men and women between the ages of 35 and 47. They found that 27 percent of the subjects that averaged 5 hours of sleep per night had plaque in their coronary arteries (the arteries of the heart itself), compared with just 6 percent of those who slept more than 7 hours per night. At the time, the researchers were unsure why this happened. However, another study, which was published in 2016, suggested that it was because lack of sleep interfered with the body's ability to break down cholesterol—the material that forms plaque. Other studies have found a link between lack of sleep and development of Alzheimer's disease later in life, although more research is required to prove this link.

Diabetes is a disease that affects the body's ability to regulate glucose, or blood sugar. If left untreated or treated incorrectly, it can lead to kidney failure and blindness. There are two types of diabetes. The first one, type 1, is an autoimmune disorder, which means the immune system makes a mistake and begins attacking healthy body parts. In the case of diabetes, the body attacks cells in the pancreas that produce insulin, a substance that controls glucose levels. No one is entirely sure why some people develop autoimmune diseases.

Type 2 diabetes is far more common, and it is not an autoimmune disease. It happens when a person's pancreas stops producing insulin. It has been linked to sleep deprivation; a number of studies have shown that sleeping four hours or less for as little as two nights can affect the body's ability to produce insulin. Once individuals get enough sleep, insulin production returns to normal. If sleep deprivation becomes chronic, however, insulin production stays disrupted, and blood sugar levels can rise to abnormal levels, putting people at risk of developing diabetes.

Type 2 diabetes is also associated with obesity, and lack of sleep has been shown to lead to weight gain. Sleep deprivation can lower the production of an appetite-suppressing hormone known as leptin while boosting an appetite-inducing hormone known as ghrelin. As a result, some sleep-deprived individuals eat more than well-rested individuals. A 2011 study at New York's Columbia University showed that subjects who slept for 4 hours a night for 5 nights ate 300 more calories per day than did subjects who slept for 9 hours. The study also found that the sleep-deprived subjects craved calorie-laden junk food. A 2007 University of Chicago study had almost identical findings. According to University of Chicago researcher Eve Van Cauter,

> *Subjects who had the most disrupted levels of leptin and ghrelin were the ones who felt the hungriest. Their appetite for cakes, candy, ice cream, potato chips, pasta, and bread increased, though their appetite for fruits, vegetables, and high-protein nutrients did not. We don't know why food choice would shift, but since the brain is fueled by glucose, we suspect it seeks simple carbohydrates when distressed by lack of sleep.*[10]

People who do not get enough sleep are more likely to crave foods that are bad for them, which can lead to further health problems.

Other, more recent studies have found similar results. To make matters worse, lack of sleep leaves people too tired to work off the extra calories they consume, and, according to a 2011 study at Sweden's Uppsala University, sleep deprivation slows down individuals' waking metabolism, which means they burn fewer calories.

On the basis of these findings, it is not surprising to learn that a number of other studies have shown that sleep deprivation is associated with obesity. For instance, a Columbia University study that tracked

6,115 adults found that subjects who slept an average of 4 hours per night were 73 percent more likely to be obese than those who slept 7 to 9 hours. More than 30 other studies have found a strong connection between short sleep duration in children and future obesity. In the last 50 years, the incidence of obesity has more than doubled in the United States, while sleep time has also been reduced. Some sleep researchers think there is a direct correlation. In rare cases, however, the opposite is true: Severe lack of sleep can make someone feel sick and unable to eat. These people tend to lose more weight than is healthy for them if their sleep deprivation continues for a long period of time.

Too little sleep makes it hard to concentrate on important tasks.

Lack of sleep also causes problems with the body's immune system, which helps it destroy invaders such as bacteria and viruses. A number of studies have shown that sleep deprivation reduces the production of infection-fighting T cells, making it more difficult for individuals to fight off infections. A 2009 study at Carnegie Mellon University in Pittsburgh, Pennsylvania, found that healthy test subjects who slept less than seven hours per night were almost three times more likely to become sick after being exposed to a cold virus than subjects who slept eight hours per night.

Sleep deprivation can cause issues such as difficulty concentrating or remembering things. It can also make symptoms of other illnesses worse, including attention-deficit/hyperactivity disorder (ADHD) and mental illnesses such as depression and anxiety. Although many aspects of sleep remain a mystery, it is clear that sleep is a basic need, which is why people with sleep disorders face multiple health threats. There are many different kinds of sleep disorders, so in order to treat them, it is important to distinguish between these different kinds.

CHAPTER TWO

THE EFFECTS OF SLEEP DISORDERS

Scientists have identified dozens of different sleep disorders, and it is possible for someone to have more than one. The *International Classification of Sleep Disorders* (*ICSD*) was first published in 1990 to help doctors identify and diagnose different sleep disorders. As of 2019, it is in its third edition.

The *ICSD-3* identifies six major categories of sleep disorders: insomnia, sleep-related breathing disorders, central disorders of hypersomnolence, circadian rhythm sleep-wake disorders, parasomnias, and sleep-related movement disorders.

Insomnia: A Common Problem

Insomnia is the most common of all sleep disorders. People with insomnia have problems falling asleep, staying asleep, or getting high-quality sleep. To be diagnosed with insomnia, a person must be unable to sleep even if they have the opportunity and circumstances for it. In other words, if someone is kept awake by loud noises or bright lights, they do not have insomnia, they just have poor sleeping conditions. Furthermore, a diagnosis of insomnia requires someone to be impaired during the day by their lack of sleep.

Insomnia can be temporary, lasting from one day to three weeks. This type of insomnia is generally caused by excitement or worry before a major event in a person's life, a temporary illness that disrupts sleep, or a

Insomnia can cause distress as people try and fail to fall asleep, knowing how tired they will be the next day.

single ongoing stressful situation. Once the illness, worry, stress, or excitement passes, individuals quickly return to normal sleep patterns.

Insomnia that occurs on most nights for at least a month is known as chronic insomnia. Chronic insomnia can trouble people for much of their lives. As one middle-aged person with insomnia noted, "I can't remember EVER being able to sleep! … As a child I remember being the ONLY one awake at slumber parties. I don't know how I made it in college on such little sleep."[11]

Exact numbers of chronic insomnia sufferers are difficult to come by, but it is known to be a common problem. In many cases, chronic insomnia arises as a symptom of another sleep disorder or long-term health problem that interferes with sleep, such as anxiety or depression. It can also occur as a side effect of medications that suppress sleep. This is known as secondary insomnia. Cases of chronic insomnia that are not linked to other conditions are known as primary insomnia.

Experts do not know what causes primary insomnia. Some cases seem to run in families, but no specific genes linked to the condition have been identified. Other cases are associated with poor sleep habits; changes in the body, such as hormonal changes that happen during menstruation; or long-term stress.

The causes of primary insomnia can be divided into three categories:

- **psychophysiological insomnia:** A period of stress or a change in work pattern, such as moving to an overnight shift, causes someone to adopt poor sleeping habits. These habits are reinforced over time, so "the person 'learns' to worry about his or her sleep, and sleeplessness continues for years after the stress has subsided. Therefore, it is also called learned insomnia or behavioral insomnia."[12]
- **idiopathic insomnia:** There is no known cause. Some researchers believe it is due to problems in the brain, but this has not yet been proven.
- **sleep state misperception:** The person feels as if they have insomnia but shows no symptoms of it.

Insomnia can occur at the beginning of sleep. This is known as sleep onset insomnia. Although most people fall asleep in about 15 minutes, it can take hours for people with sleep onset insomnia to fall asleep. Many people who have it say they have trouble turning off their minds. As soon as they shut their eyes, they are troubled by feelings of anxiety, including anxiety about not being able to fall asleep. As one person with insomnia explained, "Just the thought of going to bed starts the anxiety all over again. Clock-watching is my night, struggling to stay awake is my day. Why can't I turn off my brain when I go to bed?"[13] People with this type of insomnia tend to spend more time in less-refreshing N1 sleep than other sleepers. Many misinterpret the light N1 sleep for wakefulness, thinking that they have not slept when they actually have.

Some people with insomnia wake up frequently during the night and find it difficult to fall back to sleep. Since repeated awakenings disrupt normal sleep cycles, these individuals do not get good-quality sleep. This is known as middle insomnia.

People with terminal insomnia sleep well until about 3 a.m., when they awaken and are unable to get back to sleep. Since REM sleep increases as the night goes on, this type of insomnia reduces the time spent in REM sleep. In addition to feeling the effects of sleep deprivation the next day, many of these individuals report problems with their memory. It is most common in the elderly, people who have depression, and women who are going through menopause—a period of time marked by hormonal changes and the permanent end of a woman's menstruation.

Sleep and Breathing Problems

People with sleep-related breathing disorders experience pauses in their breathing during sleep, causing reduced oxygen levels in the blood. Sleep-related breathing disorders are almost as common as insomnia. The most common one, which is called obstructive sleep apnea (OSA), is the second most common sleep disorder. It affects more than 18 million American adults.

There are three types of sleep apnea—central, obstructive, and mixed sleep apnea. In central sleep apnea, the brain fails to control breathing during sleep. There are multiple subsets of it, such as central sleep apnea due to medication or substance abuse, but overall, central sleep apnea is rare. Generally, when medical professionals talk about sleep apnea, they are talking about obstructive sleep apnea, which is caused by a blockage, or obstruction, of the airway in the throat. Muscles throughout the body relax during sleep. In people with OSA, the throat muscles become so relaxed that they collapse, causing them or the tongue to temporarily block the flow of air in and out of the lungs.

People with OSA stop breathing for intervals of 10 seconds or more while they are asleep. This causes

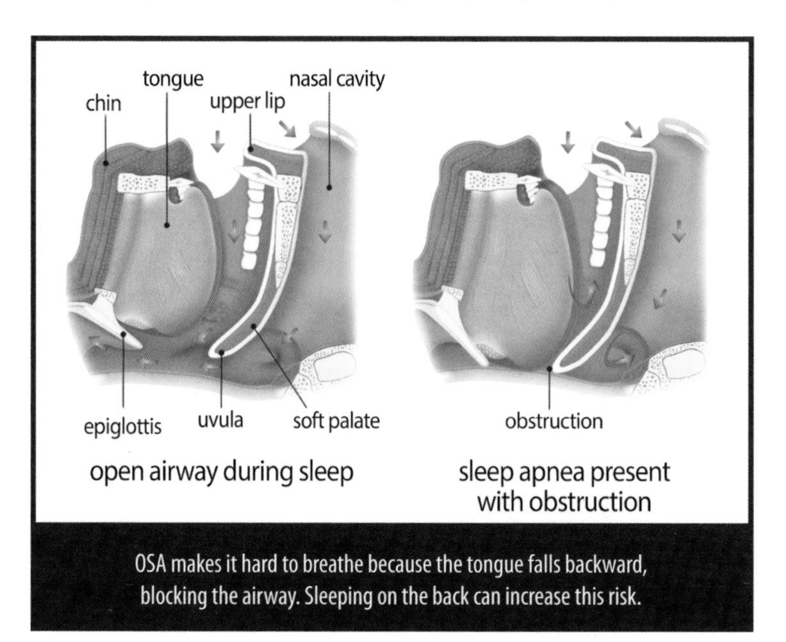

OSA makes it hard to breathe because the tongue falls backward, blocking the airway. Sleeping on the back can increase this risk.

them to wake up for a few seconds to catch their breath. These episodes occur multiple times in a night. OSA is considered mild if someone has 5 to 14 episodes per hour, moderate if they experience 15 to 30 episodes per hour, and severe if they experience more than 30 per hour. Although some individuals have trouble going back to sleep, most fall back to sleep without being aware of what happened. Frequent awakenings, however, cause individuals with OSA to spend more time in N1 sleep than is normal and less time in the more restorative N3. This is one reason why they feel very tired the next day. In fact, many people with sleep apnea report falling asleep at inappropriate times during the day. Mike, a man who was diagnosed with sleep apnea, recalled,

> *For years I had been getting sleepier and sleepier. I went to bed early, but woke up the next morning feeling dragged out and unrested. I used to sit on the edge of the bed in the morning and count the hours till I could take a nap. I fell asleep at work … I fell asleep during the 5 o'clock news. I dragged*

off to bed at 8:30 or 9:00 at night and woke up the next morning to start the whole thing all over.[14]

A third, rare type of sleep apnea that has not been thoroughly studied as of 2019 is called mixed, or complex, sleep apnea. This combines the symptoms of both central and obstructive sleep apnea. According to the Alaska Sleep Clinic, "In 2006 researchers from the Mayo Clinic conducted a study of 223 sleep apnea patients and found that 15% of sleep apnea patients who were believed to have OSA in fact had mixed sleep apnea."[15]

Often, sleep apnea patients are unaware that they have the condition. People who share a room with them, such as siblings, roommates, or friends at a sleepover, are generally the first to notice an issue. As people with sleep apnea struggle to breathe, they produce extremely loud snores, followed by silence when they stop breathing and then a gasp for air. Snoring associated with sleep apnea is much louder and more

A Traveler's Sleep Disorder

Jet lag is a feeling of extreme tiredness that occurs when people cross multiple time zones quickly. It is a circadian rhythm disorder in which a traveler's circadian clock functions on the light-dark sleep time of their place of origin, rather than on that of the place they traveled to. This puts them out of sync with the local time. For instance, a traveler going from New York City to London, England, crosses five time zones. If the traveler leaves New York at 5 p.m. and arrives in London 7 hours later, the traveler's circadian clock, which is on New York time, thinks it is 12 a.m. The time in London, however, is 5 a.m., nearly time to wake up and start the day.

Symptoms of jet lag include sleepiness, headaches, insomnia, memory problems, digestive upsets, and irritability. Jet lag is a temporary condition that corrects itself as the brain gradually adjusts its circadian clock. According to the Alaska Sleep Clinic, "As a general rule of thumb, when traveling east it takes about one day of recovery for each time zone crossed, and half the amount of time for westward travel."[1] Travelers can deal with jet lag by trying to adjust their sleep schedule before they leave for their trip, drinking plenty of water, and avoiding alcohol and caffeine.

1. Kevin Phillips, "What Is Jet Lag? Causes, Symptoms, & Treatments for Jet Lag," Alaska Sleep Clinic, November 26, 2014. www.alaskasleep.com/blog/jet-lag-sleep-disorder-symptoms-treatment-travel-fatigue.

regular than the snores of healthy sleepers. Often, this nighttime noise and the choking gasps that come with it awaken family members, who alert the sleeper to the problem.

Certain physical characteristics put someone at a higher risk for developing sleep apnea. These include crowded airways caused by enlarged tonsils or adenoids (tissue between the back of the nose and throat), a large tongue, a wide neck, and obesity. Excess weight can produce extra fat in the neck, which contributes to an airway blockage. It also puts pressure on the airways, reducing a person's ability to breathe during sleep. Although people with sleep apnea are not likely to suffocate, apnea episodes can cause blood oxygen levels to fall dangerously low. This causes the heart to work harder and raises blood pressure, putting people at risk of heart attack and stroke.

Other sleep-related breathing disorders include hypoventilation disorders and sleep-related hypoxemia disorder. Hypoventilation is a medical term that describes decreased breathing, leading to too much carbon dioxide in the blood. This can also cause sleep-related hypoxemia, which is a condition in which there is too little oxygen in the blood. According to the American Sleep Association, "A person will naturally adjust to hypoventilation while awake, taking deeper and/or longer breaths as needed. During episodes of apnea though … this can lead to dangerously high levels of carbon dioxide in the blood."[16] In rare, serious cases, a person can die from this condition. Most cases of hypoventilation are caused by other medical problems that make breathing difficult, such as bronchitis, but in rare cases, the cause is unknown, as the lungs look normal and there is no other disease present. Symptoms include headaches, heart problems, stomach problems, daytime sleepiness, and feeling faint.

When Movement Disrupts Sleep

Sleep-related movement disorders, as the name suggests, involve simple involuntary movements that make it difficult for individuals to fall and stay asleep. Restless legs syndrome is the most common. People with restless legs syndrome complain of mild to severe tingling, burning, and aching in their legs, which generally begins at night and ends in the morning. The feeling can only be relieved by moving or putting pressure on the legs. As a result, people with this syndrome are sleep deprived, and what sleep they do get is poor quality. About 10 percent of American adults and 2 percent of American children experience restless legs syndrome, but it is often misdiagnosed as insomnia, muscle cramps, arthritis, or anxiety.

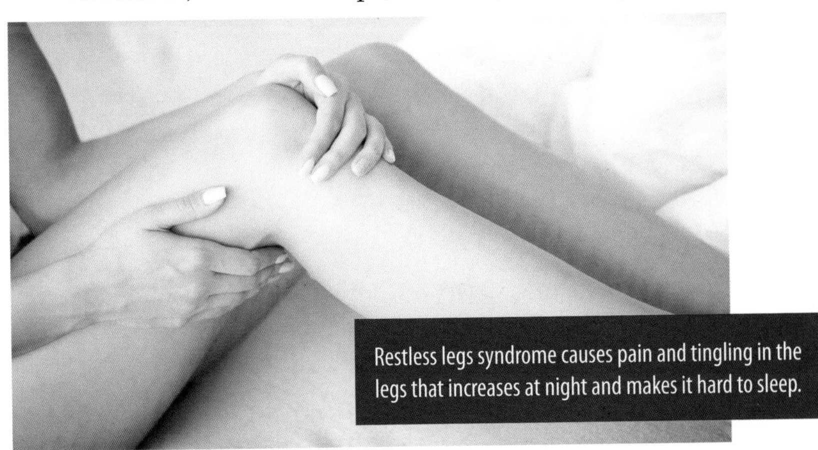

Restless legs syndrome causes pain and tingling in the legs that increases at night and makes it hard to sleep.

In 2007, scientists at Emory University in Atlanta, Georgia, identified a gene that makes individuals more likely to develop restless legs syndrome, and up to half of people who have the syndrome also have family members who have it. However, genetics does not appear to be the only cause. Some pregnant women develop the condition during pregnancy, but the symptoms generally disappear after they give birth. Some cases seem to be linked to anemia, a medical condition characterized by an iron deficiency. Scientists theorize that a lack of iron causes brain signals to misfire, resulting in the symptoms of restless legs syndrome. Some medications can also cause or worsen the syndrome.

Sleep-related leg cramps are similar but are classified as a different disorder because they are not constant, the way the feelings are in restless legs syndrome. Leg cramps occur when the calf muscles tighten, and they can be so painful that they wake people up in the middle of the night. They can be caused by certain medications, neurological problems, or pregnancy, and more women than men report having them. Very few studies have been done on this issue, so there are no medical treatments for leg cramps that are both safe and effective. In the absence of medical studies, some people turn to unscientific folk remedies to try to relieve their pain. For instance, some—but not all—people have reported relief from a bizarre source: an unwrapped bar of soap placed under the sheets. No one knows why this helps some people, but one theory is that the soap gives off the chemical magnesium, and low magnesium is a known cause of muscle cramps. People may also see results from taking a magnesium supplement or eating more foods that are rich in magnesium, such as almonds, avocados, tofu, bananas, and dark chocolate.

Many people with leg cramps and restless legs syndrome have reported relief from putting a bar of soap in their bed, although there is no scientific evidence behind it.

Another common disorder that is classified as a sleep-related movement disorder is called sleep-related bruxism, which is the medical term for unconsciously grinding or clenching the teeth. If left untreated, it can cause severe damage to teeth as well as jaw pain. The exact cause is unknown, but evidence suggests it is related to "sleep related arousals in which the cardiac and respiratory systems show a rise in activity. These arousals can take place up to 15 times an hour during sleep. Arousals during sleep are often accompanied by increased muscle activity such as in the jaw, which can be a source of teeth grinding."[17] It can also be caused by stress and anxiety.

Parasomnias

Sleep disorders known as parasomnias also involve movement. Individuals with a parasomnia perform involuntary physical activities that range from sitting up in bed to walking, talking, eating, screaming, and even driving while asleep. All parasomnias disrupt sleep and normal sleep cycles.

Experts do not know what causes parasomnias. They believe something goes wrong in the sleeper's brain as it moves in or out of N3, causing part of the brain to become partially awake while another part is in deep sleep. This puts sleepers in a situation where they are not fully awake nor fully asleep. It allows them to perform physical activities associated with wakefulness that they do not remember doing upon awakening.

It is difficult to awaken sleepers during a parasomnia episode. If sleepers are awakened, they are likely to be confused. In some cases—especially for sleepwalkers—it is dangerous to do so because sleepwalkers have been known to attack the person waking them in their confusion. It is a myth, however, that a person who is awakened while sleepwalking might suffer a heart attack from fright. Experts say the best thing to do is try to lead the sleepwalker back to bed without waking them. If a sleepwalker must be awakened for their safety, Sleep.org recommends using "loud, sharp noises (from a safe distance) to wake up the person"[18] instead of shaking or poking them in a way that might make them feel they are being attacked.

Sleepwalking can be dangerous because sleepwalkers have no awareness or control over their activities. They have only limited awareness of their environment, and their coordination and judgment are poor. Sleepwalkers have been known to urinate in inappropriate places, wander aimlessly outdoors, light fires, drive vehicles, and fall out of windows. Some sleepwalkers may prepare food and eat during a sleepwalking episode; this is classified as a type of parasomnia called sleep-related eating disorders. These people tend to eat high-calorie foods in ways they generally avoid during the day—for example, they may drink maple syrup straight from the bottle. They may also eat strange or unhealthy items, "such as raw bacon, buttered cigarettes, or coffee grounds … [or] toxic substances, such as cleaning solutions."[19]

However, sleepwalking episodes can also be harmless; people may simply wander into another room and sit down or talk to someone for a few minutes and then walk back to bed. Sleep talking also does not pose a danger to the sleeper and can result in some stories that even the sleep talker finds amusing. In movies and TV shows, sleep talking is often used as a way to give the audience or another character information; for example, a sleeper may say something that reveals a deep secret. In reality, however, sleep talkers tend to say things that sound like random nonsense.

A parasomnia called REM sleep behavior disorder, which is similar to sleepwalking, causes people to act out their dreams, as their muscles do not become paralyzed during REM sleep to prevent them from doing so. Sleepwalkers are less likely to remember what they

In the media, sleepwalkers are often shown with their arms outstretched and their eyes closed. In reality, they generally look as if they are awake, walking around normally with their eyes open.

were dreaming about than people with REM sleep behavior disorder; additionally, sleepwalkers' eyes are generally open, while people who have REM sleep behavior disorder typically have their eyes closed while acting out their dreams.

Both adults and children suffer from parasomnias, but certain types of parasomnias, such as sleep terrors or night terrors, occur most often in children. People having night terrors show signs of panic while sleeping: Their hearts pound, their breathing accelerates, they scream in fear, and they sweat more than normal. Most episodes last only a couple minutes, but it can take up to half an hour for someone to calm down and fall back asleep. However, the person often does not wake up at all and simply returns to a calm sleeping state as if nothing happened. Night terrors are different than nightmares; most people remember a nightmare when they wake up, but people who experience night terrors are generally unaware of what has happened. As with sleep apnea, it is generally the other people in the house—whose sleep is also disrupted when they are awakened by screams—who let them know there is an issue. Most children eventually outgrow night terrors, and experts say there is no need to seek treatment unless they are happening regularly, causing daytime sleepiness, or leading to unsafe sleepwalking episodes.

Night terrors are more common in children than in adults.

Circadian Rhythm Sleep-Wake Disorders

Circadian rhythm sleep-wake disorders are another form of sleep disorder. These disorders are caused by a mismatch between the body's circadian clock and the external environment. Delayed sleep-wake phase disorder is among the most common circadian rhythm sleep-wake disorder. In this disorder, individuals' circadian clocks run behind that of the external environment. People with this disorder do not feel sleepy until 1 a.m. or later, instead of a more normal time, such as 10 p.m. Some do not feel sleepy until dawn. They therefore have trouble waking up in the morning and functioning on a normal schedule. Additionally, since their sleep period is shortened, they get less REM sleep than they need.

About 5 to 10 percent of teenagers have this disorder. During puberty, hormonal changes in a teen's body cause their circadian rhythm to shift slightly, resulting in delays in the time they are ready to go to bed and the time they are ready to wake up. Scientists think an unknown gene—or, more likely, multiple genes—may cause this shift to be more severe in some teens. The shift generally normalizes as teens become adults and hormone levels stabilize. However, many teens stay up late using computers, playing video games, texting, and watching TV. These activities expose users to blue light, which causes the body to suppress the release of melatonin. Over time, this behavior can prevent the person's circadian rhythm from stabilizing and may delay it even further.

Delayed sleep-wake phase disorder can be caused by a problem with the body's circadian clock. However, most cases are caused by people voluntarily staying up late, night after night, until this behavior causes their circadian clock to reset. Similar disorders include advanced sleep-wake phase disorder, in which someone falls asleep in the late afternoon or early evening and wakes up around 3:00 a.m.; irregular sleep-wake rhythm disorder, in which the times a person feels sleepy and alert do not follow any consistent pattern; and shift work disorder, in which a person who works irregular job shifts throws their circadian clock out of rhythm.

Central Disorders of Hypersomnolence

Hypersomnolence—the medical term for sleeping too much—can cause excessive daytime sleepiness. Sometimes it is caused by medications or as a side effect of another medical problem. However, narcolepsy is the most common type of hypersomnolence, or hypersomnia. It affects 1 in 2,000 Americans. In the past, medical professionals believed narcolepsy was a form of mental illness, but research has proven this wrong. It is unknown exactly what causes narcolepsy, but scientists suspect it is "a combination of genetic and environmental factors that influence the immune system."[20] Patients with narcolepsy have been found to have severely reduced levels of hypocretin, a neurotransmitter (brain chemical) that helps people stay awake. It is believed that this is because the immune system attacks hypocretin-producing cells in the brain. However, more research must be done to prove this theory.

Unusual Sleep Disorders

Some sleep disorders are very rare and have unusual symptoms. Some of these rare disorders include:

- Kleine-Levin syndrome: People with this disorder sleep up to 23 hours per day for up to 3 weeks in a row and are difficult to awaken. It mainly affects young men around the age of 15, and the symptoms last for about 8 years. According to the Alaska Sleep Clinic, "when they do wake they often exhibit unusual and excessive behaviors such as: binge eating, compulsive behaviors … confusion, apathy, hallucinations, and sometimes childlike behaviors."[1] The cause is unknown, but it has been linked to an infection. The only medication that currently controls it is lithium, a mood stabilizer that is typically prescribed for people with bipolar disorder.
- exploding head syndrome: This disorder causes people to hallucinate loud noises that wake them up just as they are starting to fall asleep. The sounds have been compared to cymbal crashes, gunshots, and slamming doors. Some people also hallucinate a bright light at the same time. This disorder does not cause pain, but it does cause people to panic at the unexpected noise and can lead to sleep-onset insomnia.
- fatal familial insomnia: In this sleep disorder, a person's inability to sleep increases steadily until within a few months, sleep is no longer possible at all. However, "lack of sleep itself is not what proves to be deadly for the sufferers but rather other symptoms that begin to manifest themselves shortly after they begin to lose the ability to go to sleep. The body begins … having difficulty controlling blood pressure, heart rate, and body temperature."[2] Fortunately, very few people ever develop this disorder. Someone experiencing sleeplessness, even over a long period of time, likely has normal insomnia.

1. Jennifer Hines, "5 Strange and Terrifying Sleep Disorders," Alaska Sleep Clinic, June 8, 2018. www.alaskasleep.com/blog/5-strange-and-terrifying-sleep-disorders.

2. Hines, "5 Strange and Terrifying Sleep Disorders."

People with narcolepsy experience microsleeps and have uncontrollable attacks of daytime sleepiness that give them a strong urge to fall asleep at inappropriate times. These urges are called sleep attacks and can occur multiple times throughout the day without warning. As Stephanie Handy, a woman with narcolepsy, explained,

> *During a sleep attack I find that my eyes will not stay open … As sleep comes, suddenly I can feel my neck and head slump onto my shoulder. My arms are relaxed and weakened. I may attempt to sit or "fall" into the chair, sometimes injuring myself when sitting or laying down since I have decreased ability to control my descent. These attacks cause me a lot of grief … I've had them at concerts, movies, watching TV, playing video games … I don't know of any activity I've done that hasn't been interrupted by a sleep attack at some time in my life.*[21]

Narcolepsy also affects nightly sleep. When people with narcolepsy go to sleep at night, rather than going through a normal sleep cycle, they almost immediately fall into REM sleep. This disruption in their sleep cycle decreases the quality of their sleep and causes them to wake frequently during the night. Since they skip the initial stages of sleep and begin their sleep in REM, their brains do not shift fully into sleep mode. As a result, during the time that people with narcolepsy shift from wakefulness to sleep and vice versa, their dreams often seem like they are actually happening, much like a hallucination. They may also be aware of the paralysis that accompanies REM sleep, a condition called sleep paralysis. Sleep paralysis is relatively common; about 50 percent of people around the world

Some animals can have narcolepsy, although it is much more rare than it is in people. Shown here is Mable, a dog that experiences narcolepsy symptoms when it gets excited.

have experienced it, although only about 4 percent of people have more than 5 episodes in their lifetime. They report having frightening hallucinations, feelings of panic, and shortness of breath. Sleep paralysis is so common, in fact, that it has given rise to legends that are shared by multiple cultures. Most people with sleep paralysis hallucinate shadowy figures standing in a corner of their room or sitting on their chest; these creatures have been named things such as "shadow man" and "night hag," and some cultures believe they are evil spirits that visit people at night. Some experts also believe that sleep paralysis might be responsible for stories of alien abductions.

Because they sometimes slip into REM sleep even when they are not trying to sleep, some people with narcolepsy are subjected to this temporary paralysis while they are fully conscious. This is known as cataplexy. "Imagine a puppet on strings and suddenly the strings, which are your muscle tone, are immediately let go and so you fall to the ground,"[22] explained Bob Cloud, a patient with cataplexy.

Cataplexy is triggered by strong emotions such as fear, joy, or anger and is similar to the temporary paralysis of the skeletal muscles that occurs during REM sleep. Attacks are unpredictable; they may occur dozens of times in one week and hardly at all the next. Whenever the attacks occur, they put people at risk of serious injury. Handy recalled, "I was happily roller skating near my house when my knees suddenly buckled … When I hit the ground, I fractured my wrist. Fully conscious, I was unable to do anything."[23]

Clearly, sleep disorders cause many problems. The first step in dealing with these problems is getting an accurate diagnosis so treatment can begin.

CHAPTER THREE

DIAGNOSIS AND TREATMENT

The first step in diagnosing a sleep disorder is a physical exam. This helps doctors diagnose or rule out other health conditions that may be interfering with sleep. They also run certain tests to figure out which sleep disorder the person is experiencing. For example, a blood test can help diagnose narcolepsy by showing whether the person has the specific genes that have been linked to a higher risk of developing the disorder. Many people must undergo a sleep study as part of the diagnostic process. This is when the person spends the night at a sleep center so doctors can monitor how they are sleeping. They do this not only by observing the patient for signs of disorders such as sleep apnea, but also by attaching monitoring machines to check things such as oxygen levels and brain activity.

Undergoing a Sleep Study

When sleep problems affect a person's daily life, it is time to see a sleep specialist—a physician who specializes in treating sleep disorders. Before the visit, patients are generally asked to record information about their sleep history in a sleep log, or journal. This information helps physicians better understand the patient's sleep troubles.

During the first visit, the doctor checks for illnesses that can cause secondary insomnia and examines the patient's airways and mouth for signs of enlarged

During a sleep study, sensors are applied to a person's skin to monitor what is happening while they are asleep.

tonsils, adenoids, or tongue, which can cause sleep apnea. The doctor questions the patient about any emotional problems that might be affecting sleep. If a sleep disorder is suspected, the patient is typically asked to spend the night at a sleep center. An overnight sleep study is called a polysomnogram. There are also two types of daytime sleep studies: a multiple sleep latency test (MSLT) and a maintenance of wakefulness test (MWT). They generally follow a polysomnogram and measure how well someone is able to stay awake and alert during the day. The MSLT is especially helpful in diagnosing narcolepsy, while the MWT is essential in determining whether someone's daytime sleepiness makes them a danger to others when they drive or operate machinery.

A sleep center is a medical center where patients sleep while hooked up to equipment used to diagnose sleep disorders. Some sleep center rooms look like hospital rooms, but others look like hotel rooms. After the patient dresses in pajamas and gets into bed, a sleep technician tapes electrodes to the patient's head near the eyes, nose, and mouth, as well as to the chest, chin, and legs. This is painless. The sensors are connected by wires to a polysomnograph, a machine that includes an EEG as well as other devices that measure muscle activity, airflow from the mouth and nose, blood oxygen levels, and heartbeat. A computer converts the information into graphs. A video camera and speakers record any movements or sounds the sleeping patient makes. Sleep technicians monitor the patient and the equipment.

The accommodations are designed to encourage sleep. The bed is comfortable, and the room is kept cool, quiet, and dark. The sensors, the stress of being watched by strangers, and the unfamiliar bed and surroundings make it difficult for some patients to fall asleep, but many patients fall asleep more easily than they expect to. The Alaska Sleep Clinic explained,

> *Being able to sleep comfortably outside of one's own bed while hooked up to a myriad [massive amount] of wires may seem an impossible feat. But it's really not. Rarely does a sleep study fail because the patient was unable to sleep. Even if you think that you didn't get* any *sleep during your overnight sleep study, you may be surprised to find that you slept much more than you realized. And even if you really didn't get a whole lot of sleep during your study, chances are you slept enough to obtain an adequate amount of data.*[24]

Patients are awakened by the technicians in the morning, and they generally get the results of their test in about 10 days. People who do have a lot of difficulty falling asleep anywhere but their home or who are nervous about being watched may be able to do a home sleep study by renting or purchasing a special monitoring device they can wear at home. However, a home test can only diagnose or rule out sleep apnea—it cannot diagnose any other type of sleep disorder. Additionally, the equipment tends to have a hard time diagnosing mild to moderate sleep apnea, so a doctor may only recommend a home test if they suspect the patient has a moderate to severe case.

The Epworth Sleepiness Scale

Another tool doctors use to diagnose narcolepsy in particular is called the Epworth Sleepiness Scale. It is a simple questionnaire that patients can complete at home so they can show the results to their doctor. Patients use a scale of 0 to 3 ("would never doze" to "high chance of dozing") to rank how likely they are to fall asleep while doing certain activities, such as watching TV, driving a car, and talking to a friend. If the patient scores 10 or higher, it indicates that they may have a sleep disorder. The tool is not intended to help people diagnose themselves, but to help them consider whether they should talk to a sleep specialist about their sleeping problems. People who score greater than 10 may also be asked to answer questions on the Swiss Narcolepsy Scale, which is a five-item questionnaire with specific questions about symptoms of cataplexy.

Interpreting the Study

Sleep studies are important because they help researchers correctly diagnose the problem. It may end up not being a sleep problem at all, but some other underlying problem. For instance, ADHD is frequently confused with sleep disorders because it causes behaviors that can interfere with sleep. As an example, the ADHD magazine *ADDitude* looked at two people, Jake and Mari. Jake consistently went to bed hours later than he had planned to, giving him little time to sleep, while Mari played games on her phone until she fell asleep. Gina Pera, the article's author, explained,

> *Based on appearances alone, sleep specialists might insist that Jake and Mari don't have ADHD, despite professional diagnoses and vastly improved daytime functioning, thanks to stimulant medication. Instead, these experts might advise Jake to make a better effort to get in bed by 10 and Mari to refrain from taking her iPhone under the sheets.*

> *That way, both could have more sleep and enjoy improved cognitive ability during the day ...*
>
> *When it comes to ADHD, however, appearances can deceive. Jake's poor sense of timing is a lifelong trait ... Mari has battled "brain chatter" when trying to fall asleep since she was a child. Playing iPhone games is not the cause of her delay in going to sleep; it's her latest strategy for dealing with boredom.*[25]

People may also mistakenly be diagnosed with ADHD when their true problem is poor sleep habits. These examples show that a person's full medical history must be taken into account when diagnosing sleep disorders. Sleep studies give doctors a chance to see firsthand how someone behaves when it is time for bed, giving them more diagnostic clues.

After the sleep study, technicians score the results of the polysomnogram, using numbers and percentages. The information is divided into a number of categories, including time in bed; total sleep time; sleep time spent in each stage of sleep; sleep latency, or the time it takes the patient to fall asleep; REM latency, or the time from sleep onset to the first start of REM; number of apnea episodes per hour; blood oxygen levels; and the number of periodic limb movements that awaken the patient. The technician also reviews the video and audio recordings, noting any abnormalities, such as what sleep position patients are in when apnea episodes occur. The sleep specialist uses the scoring and the technician's notes to make a diagnosis. Once this is done, treatment can begin.

Using a CPAP Machine

Treatment for sleep disorders depends on the specific disorder and the individual. For instance, in cases of sleep apnea, overweight patients are advised to lose weight since excess fat in the neck can impair breathing. If apnea episodes occur mainly while patients sleep on their backs, patients are told to avoid sleeping in this position.

Back sleeping is a problem for many people with sleep apnea. It causes the tongue to flop backward, which can block the airway. To keep from rolling over onto their back while they are sleeping, some patients wear a tight-fitting sleep shirt with a tennis ball stuffed in the back, which makes it uncomfortable to sleep on their backs.

People with sleep apnea are also typically treated with continuous positive airway pressure (CPAP) therapy. A CPAP machine blows air through a mask that people wear when they sleep. The airflow forces the sleeper's airway to stay open during the night, reducing sleep apnea episodes. Airflow pressure is based on each patient's individual needs. In general, more severe cases need stronger air pressure than milder cases.

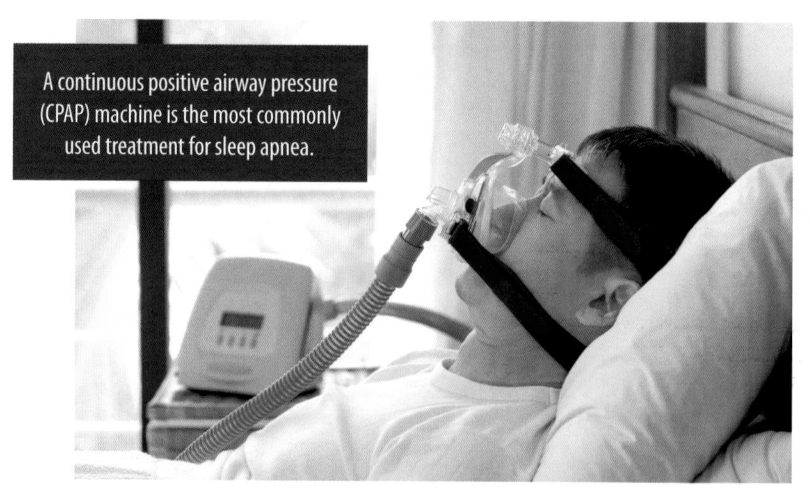

A continuous positive airway pressure (CPAP) machine is the most commonly used treatment for sleep apnea.

If a CPAP machine has to be set to a very high pressure, it can be uncomfortable for the patient and make them feel as if it is hard for them to breathe out. In this case, they may benefit from a bilevel positive airway pressure (BiPAP) machine. The only difference between the two is that CPAP machines have only one pressure setting and BiPAP machines have two—a higher one for inhalation, which keeps the airway open so the person can breathe, and a lower one for exhalation, so the person does not feel suffocated.

Some CPAP machines cover just the nose, while others cover both the mouth and nose. Doctors work with patients to find the most effective and comfortable mask for each individual. CPAP therapy is 99 percent effective for patients who use it on a nightly basis. However, many patients do not stick with the treatment. They report having trouble adjusting to sleeping with the mask on, to the cool air blowing against their faces, and to the whooshing sound the blower makes. Despite these drawbacks, when patients commit to the therapy, it can change their lives. As a sleep apnea sufferer named Bill explained,

> *It's been a little over a month since I started using a CPAP and I have been sleeping much better and will not sleep without my CPAP machine. It has enabled me to watch TV shows and not fall asleep. I also feel like I have more energy and walked to the store (a five to ten minute walk one way) whereas before I would have driven my truck.*
>
> *Since using the CPAP I feel like I have* much *more energy!*[26]

The treatment also decreases the person's risk of developing the heart problems that are common in people with sleep apnea.

Additional Treatments

Because people find CPAP machines uncomfortable at first, many people do not give themselves time to

An Actress's Death

Actress Carrie Fisher was best known for her role as Leia in the *Star Wars* movies, and she was also well-known as an outspoken advocate for better treatment of people with mental illnesses. However, many people were unaware that she had sleep apnea. Fisher suffered a fatal heart attack in December 2016, and her assistant stated in an interview that it was normal for her to experience apneas while sleeping. The official cause of death was listed as "sleep apnea with other conditions: atherosclerotic heart disease, drug use."[1]

Carrie Fisher's death was attributed partially to her sleep apnea.

In a statement after Fisher's death, the American Sleep Apnea Association wrote,

> *It's unclear to the American Sleep Apnea Association (ASAA) whether Fisher had been diagnosed with and/or was actively treating her sleep apnea. We are attempting to learn more so that we may help educate others about diagnosis of and treatments for this very common medical condition.*[2]

The organization also stated that it would begin a new initiative to prevent and find a cure for sleep apnea.

1. Quoted in "Yes, You Can Die from Sleep Apnea. Carrie Fisher Did," American Sleep Apnea Association, June 21, 2017. www.sleepapnea.org/carrie-fisher-yes-you-can-die-from-sleep-apnea/.

2. "Yes, You Can Die from Sleep Apnea. Carrie Fisher Did," American Sleep Apnea Association.

get used to them and tend to discontinue using them. For this reason, experts have looked at other types of treatment. In 2013, researchers at the University of Groningen in the Netherlands found that for many patients, oral appliance therapy is just as effective as CPAP therapy. Oral appliance therapy involves wearing a mouthpiece similar to a retainer or mouth guard that keeps the airway open. This type of therapy was effective for mild to moderate cases of sleep apnea; for

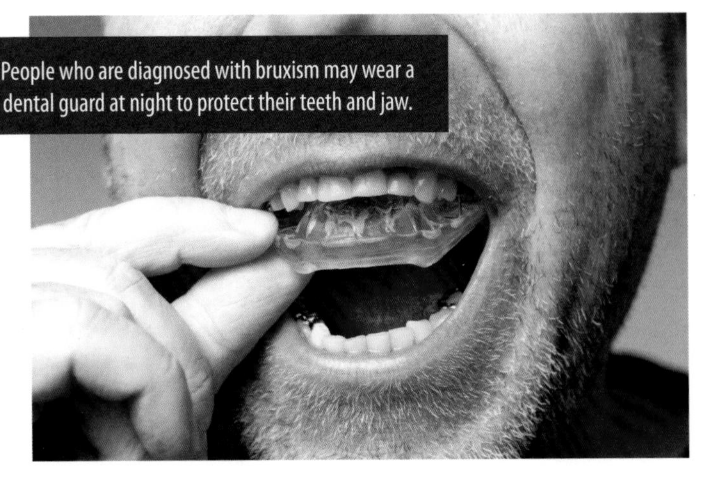
People who are diagnosed with bruxism may wear a dental guard at night to protect their teeth and jaw.

severe cases, the researchers said CPAP therapy was still the best option. If even CPAP does not work, or if the patient is having trouble wearing their device consistently, surgery is available as a last resort to remove the tonsils and extra tissue from the top of the throat.

Patients with bruxism generally also wear an oral appliance called a dental guard. These are generally made of plastic and fit over some or all of the patient's upper or lower teeth. Dental guards provide a cushion between the upper and lower teeth, reducing teeth grinding and protecting the teeth and jaw.

People with circadian rhythm sleep-wake disorders are often prescribed light therapy to help them reset their circadian clocks. Light therapy involves the use of a light box—a device that gives off light that resembles sunlight. Light boxes look like small LED panels and come in many designs. Patients sit in front of the light for a specific amount of time at specific times of day. The exact timing depends on which disorder the person has and how severe it is. It can take up to two weeks to see results. Although people can buy their own light boxes, experts recommend that light therapy only be carried out under the supervision of a trained sleep specialist. Another option, which can be used instead of or along with light therapy, is called chronotherapy. This word, which means "time therapy," describes adjusting bedtime by an hour or two to fit a normal sleep schedule. Within a few months, if the person sticks to the new schedule, their circadian clock should reset.

Using Medication

Some sleep disorders are so severe that they require medication, at least temporarily. The type of medication depends on the disorder and the patient's symptoms. For instance, stimulants—drugs that promote wakefulness and counteract daytime sleepiness—are often prescribed for people with narcolepsy. Many of these are amphetamines, which are also prescribed for people with ADHD. They work well to keep people awake and alert but can have negative side effects such as anxiety, nausea, hair loss, and increased heart rate. They can also be addictive. Non-amphetamine stimulants such as Ritalin (methylphenidate) and Provigil (modafinil) are less powerful and have shorter-lasting effects, but they also have fewer side effects. It often takes some experimentation before people find the medication that works best for them. Patients with narcolepsy who have symptoms of REM intrusion—including cataplexy, hallucinations, and sleep paralysis—may be prescribed an antidepressant medication. Antidepressants are primarily prescribed to control depression, but they also suppress REM sleep to stop it from interfering with a person's waking hours.

For insomnia, there are dozens of pills that make someone sleepy, either as a main effect or a side effect. For example, many over-the-counter (OTC) medications make people sleepy, although experts do not recommend taking them on a regular basis, as they can make it harder for someone to fall asleep without them. Other medications require a prescription and are made specifically to help people fall asleep. These include Ambien (zolpidem) and Lunesta (eszopiclone). Sometimes these are called Z-drugs because most of them start with that letter.

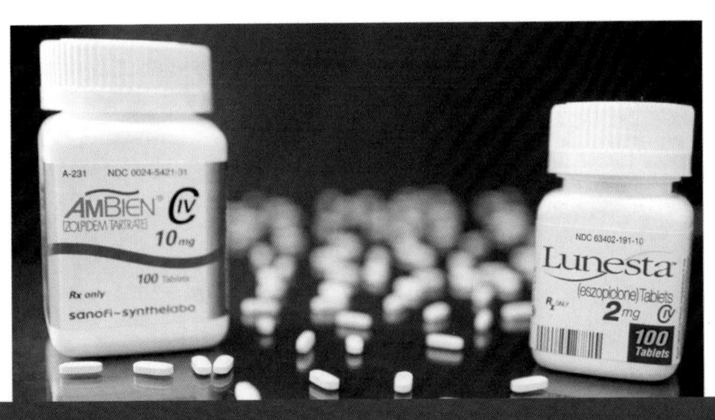

Medications such as Ambien may help people fall asleep, but they have been associated with dangerous sleepwalking episodes, so experts caution people against using them too often.

Although Z-drugs can help people fall asleep quickly, they have unusual and sometimes dangerous effects on some patients' behavior. Patients who did not previously have a parasomnia have reported bizarre episodes such as eating, cooking, driving, internet shopping, committing crimes, and setting fires while under the influence of Z-drugs.

Like OTC sleep medications, prescription sleep medications are only recommended for short-term use. When individuals take them nightly for more than four weeks, they can build up a tolerance to the medication, so they need a higher dose to get the same effect. If they try to stop taking the medication suddenly, they may experience withdrawal symptoms such as sweating, shaking, nausea, panic attacks, and muscle spasms. If combined with certain other medications, OTC or prescription sleep aids can have unintended negative side effects, and if someone takes too many or takes them too late at night, they may be drowsy the next day, which can interfere with important tasks.

A doctor can determine if a prescription sleep medication is necessary. In general, experts prefer to help people use non-drug treatments for insomnia.

Therapy and Mindfulness

If someone has insomnia because of a mental illness such as anxiety or depression, treating the underlying cause with therapy can help them find relief. In sessions with a psychologist, patients can learn a variety of techniques that are used to correct their sleep patterns. Relaxation training is among these. Relaxation training includes practicing deep breathing at bedtime, which calms the body and lessens feelings of anxiety associated with not being able to sleep. Visualization, or mindfulness, is another relaxation practice. In visualization, individuals substitute pleasant images of themselves relaxing and falling asleep for stressful images that keep them awake. Mindfulness can also be a useful technique for people with narcolepsy—for example, they may spend time in the morning visualizing themselves staying awake and alert throughout the day.

Sleep restriction therapy is another technique some people find helpful. It improves patients' sleep efficiency, or the percentage of time spent in bed asleep. For example, if a person spends 8 hours in bed but only sleeps for 4 hours, their sleep efficiency is 50 percent. People without sleep problems average 90 percent sleep efficiency.

Sleep restriction therapy involves matching the amount of time spent in bed with sleep time. If individuals spend 8 hours in bed but only 5 sleeping, sleep restriction therapy restricts their time in bed to 5 hours. Since patients with insomnia often underestimate the amount of time they spend sleeping, sleep restriction therapy causes them to feel sleepier than usual. As a result, they fall asleep faster and sleep more deeply the next night. As they start sleeping better, they begin to associate their bed with sleep instead of anxiety-inducing insomnia symptoms. As sleep efficiency increases, patients increase their time in bed by 15-minute increments with the goal of reaching at least 85 percent sleep efficiency.

Stimulus control therapy also conditions patients to associate their beds with relaxation and sleep. In stimulus control therapy, patients are trained to use their bed only for sleeping. All other activities, including watching television, eating, reading, and texting, are done in another room. When patients go to bed, if they cannot fall asleep or if they wake up during the night and cannot fall back to sleep, they must move to another room until they feel sleepy. Supporters of this therapy say that associating the bedroom only with sleep helps people fall asleep more quickly and takes away much of the stress linked to insomnia.

Many people say that doing activities other than sleeping in a bed—even something as mild as reading—can make it harder to fall asleep because people will have a harder time associating their bed with sleep.

Alternative and Complementary Treatments

Traditional treatments for sleep disorders are not effective for every patient. Even if these methods do help, some individuals are uncomfortable with the health risks that certain medications pose. For this reason, many people with sleep disorders turn to alternative treatments. For many years, these treatments were not widely accepted by the traditional medical community in the United States. Some still are not, but increasingly, doctors are recommending certain vitamins, herbal remedies, and practices such as meditation and acupuncture. When alternative treatments are combined with traditional medication, it is called complementary medicine. Some people find that complementary and alternative medicine (CAM) works to control their symptoms well enough that they do not have to take any medication. For example, someone with sleep apnea may find that yoga helps them sleep better. According to Healthline, "Yoga can specifically improve your respiratory strength and encourage oxygen flow … through its various breathing exercises. As a result, yoga reduces the amount of sleep interruptions you may experience."[27] Other people may find that a combination of CAM and prescribed medication works best for them, and still others may not experience any benefits from CAM at all.

Many CAM treatments are considered safe, but someone should always talk to their doctor before they begin CAM treatments. For one thing, unlike prescription drugs, nontraditional treatments are not subject to rigorous testing and careful regulation by the U.S. Food and Drug Administration (FDA). As a result, the purity or effectiveness of the treatment or supplement may be suspect, especially in the case of treatments purchased on the internet. Some unethical sellers, who are looking only to make money off of people searching for an effective treatment, do not label their bottles correctly. As a result, someone may be taking a higher dose than they thought or unknowingly taking a substance that has different side effects than they were expecting. For example, an herb called skullcap is sometimes used to promote sleep, but some skullcap products have been found to be contaminated with the herb germander, which can harm a person's liver. Germander was not listed on the ingredients, so someone taking another medication that affects the liver would unknowingly be taking a great risk. Additionally, some CAM remedies cause dangerous side effects when they are combined with certain prescription medications. A doctor can advise a patient of which treatments to avoid in order to prevent this from happening.

One commonly used CAM remedy is melatonin. Melatonin supplements increase the levels of the hormone the brain secretes to promote sleep. The melatonin in the supplement is generally made synthetically. Melatonin supplements appear to help regulate sleeping patterns and are most effective in treating circadian rhythm disorders because they help someone stay asleep rather than fall asleep.

Herbal treatments are also popular. Herbs have been used to promote sleep for thousands of years. Teas made from chamomile or valerian root, in particular, contain chemicals that produce a calming effect that promotes sleep. They tend to produce a weaker effect than prescription or OTC sleep medications, but it may be enough to help someone with mild insomnia. They may produce similar side effects, but these, too, tend to be less severe. However, they may interact with prescribed medications in a negative way. For example, valerian root can affect how efficiently the liver breaks down other medications. When taken with another sedative, valerian root can cause someone to have a hard time waking up.

Vitamins are also a popular CAM remedy. For instance, some research suggests that supplements such as calcium, magnesium, and B vitamins can help manage narcolepsy. Magnesium supplements may also help people who experience restless legs syndrome.

No treatment, whether traditional or nontraditional, is effective for every patient because every person's body chemistry is different. The health risks or discomfort some treatments present discourage many patients from using them. Despite these drawbacks, seeking a diagnosis and experimenting with different treatments under the supervision of a health care professional is an important step in counteracting the effects of sleep disorders.

CHAPTER FOUR

LIVING WITH A SLEEP DISORDER

Medication can make a big difference in a person's sleep quality, especially in the case of a disorder such as narcolepsy or primary insomnia. However, even with a sleep disorder, it is important for people to develop good sleeping habits to avoid making the effects of the disorder worse.

Creating good sleep habits—also sometimes called "sleep hygiene"—often involves certain lifestyle changes. One of these habits is keeping a consistent sleep schedule with a regular bedtime and awakening time. This applies to both weekdays and weekends. Keeping a regular sleep schedule helps condition the brain to fall asleep at an appropriate time and helps the body's circadian clock function properly. An article on the University of Maryland Medical Center's website advises, "Do not be one of those people who allows bedtime and awakening time to drift. The body 'gets used' to falling asleep at a certain time, but only if this is relatively fixed. Even if you are retired or not working, this is an essential component of good sleeping habits."[28]

Avoiding Stimulants

Another good sleep habit is restricting consumption of stimulants—substances that make people feel awake—such as alcohol, tobacco, and caffeine. It is well-known that coffee contains caffeine, but fewer people are aware that substances such as soda and chocolate do as well. Not surprisingly, people who drink multiple caffeinated beverages per day often have insomnia. In some cases, their caffeine habit is the cause of their insomnia. In other cases, insomniacs use caffeine to energize themselves during the day, which worsens their insomnia symptoms at night. In both instances, eliminating caffeine consumption can drastically improve sleep patterns.

Many people think that drinking an alcoholic beverage before bedtime helps them sleep. Alcohol does have a sleep-inducing effect, which makes it easier for people to fall asleep at first; however, as alcohol is processed by the body, it produces a stimulant effect, which increases the time people spend awake during the night. Alcohol also disrupts normal sleep cycles and reduces REM sleep. For this reason, experts advise adults to avoid alcohol four to six hours before they go to bed.

Most people know that coffee contains caffeine, but chocolate can also contribute to keeping someone awake longer than they intended.

Another reason alcohol should be avoided before bed, according to sleep specialist Russell Rosenberg, is that it can make sleep apnea worse. He explained, "Moderate to large amounts of alcohol consumed in the evening can lead to a substantial narrowing of the airway, increasing the frequency and duration of breath holding episodes."[29]

Nicotine, a chemical found in tobacco, negatively affects sleep, too. Like alcohol, it appears to relax the person at first. Later, however, it speeds up heartbeat, raises blood pressure, quickens breathing, and increases brain-wave activity. As a result, tobacco users wake up more frequently during the night than nonusers. During these arousals, some people get up and smoke, which makes matters worse. Smoking also harms a person's airway, making it more difficult for someone with sleep apnea to breathe.

Adjusting Diet

Just as people seeking a good night's sleep restrict their alcohol, tobacco, and caffeine intake before bedtime, they also are careful about the amount and types of food they eat before bedtime. As nutrition consultant Lisa Turner explained, "The foods we eat can dramatically affect how much, and how well, we sleep. Some calm and relax, some wake up the nervous system, and some just downright wire you for the night."[30]

Eating a heavy meal shortly before bedtime can negatively affect sleep. Generally, the digestive system slows down during sleep. Eating a heavy meal at a late hour keeps the digestive system working long into the night. The results are often heartburn, gas, and nighttime visits to the bathroom, all of which cause discomfort and disrupt sleep. Also, "your body will be too busy digesting to focus on the restorative aspects of sleeping,"[31] explained nutritionist Beth Reardon. Sleep experts advise individuals with sleep disorders to eat their last big meal at least four hours before bedtime.

Foods high in fat impact sleep in a similar manner. Fatty foods take longer to digest than other foods. A 2010 University of Pennsylvania study looked at the

Eating rich, heavy foods too close to bedtime can cause uncomfortable sleep.

effect of fat intake on sleep duration in 459 women. The researchers found that the more fat the subjects ate, the less they slept.

To Nap or Not to Nap?

Avoiding long naps during the day is generally considered part of good sleep hygiene. If people sleep too much during the day, they are not tired at night. Experts advise people who cannot get through the day without napping to limit their nap times to no more than 40 minutes and to nap before 3 p.m., so they will be tired at their regular bedtime. For people with narcolepsy, experts advise taking several naps throughout the day, lasting no more than 20 minutes each. This helps them stay awake at times when it is important, such as during an exam.

The Americans with Disabilities Act (ADA) protects students with narcolepsy by requiring schools to make special accommodations to help them. These may include accommodations such as a special place to take naps or permission to occasionally stand up during class in an effort to stay awake. In a guide titled "10 Things Educators Should Know about Students with Narcolepsy," written from the perspective of a student with narcolepsy, the Narcolepsy Network wrote, "I want to stay awake [in class], but sometimes I physically can't. When this happens, it is much better if you can give me 5–10 minutes to sleep, then [discreetly] wake me. If you wake me up right away, I will probably fall back asleep immediately, or be so groggy that I can't understand the lesson."[1] Other tips include not calling the student out in front of the class to avoid embarrassing them and allowing the student to choose their own seat. Students with narcolepsy can show this guide to their teacher if the teacher seems to be having trouble understanding how narcolepsy affects the student.

1. Melissa Patterson, "10 Things Educators Should Know about Students with Narcolepsy," Narcolepsy Network, 2013. narcolepsynetwork.org/wp-content/uploads/2014/01/10-Things-Educators-Should-Know.pdf.

Sugary foods are also troublesome. Sugar produces a rapid burst of energy followed by the release of stress hormones, which have a stimulating effect on the body. Spicy foods, too, have stimulating properties that disrupt sleep. Spicy foods can also cause indigestion, which interferes with sleep. "If you eat these foods late at night, they help promote acid reflux and can disturb sleep patterns because of that," explained Dr. Elizabeth Odstrcil of Baylor University Medical Center in Dallas, Texas. She added, "Spicy foods are thought to raise body temperature and this causes more energy expenditure that's devoted to helping digest these foods instead of sleeping and your body resting."[32]

Other foods help promote sleep. Some of these foods contain tryptophan, an amino acid (protein building block) that has a calming effect on the body. Tryptophan can increase serotonin levels, which promotes sleep because insomnia has been linked to low levels of serotonin. Additionally, foods that contain melatonin—including almonds, walnuts, raspberries, and kiwis—can promote sleep as well. According to the National Sleep Foundation, for people with insomnia, "eating two kiwis before bed can increase your sleep duration by over an hour over the course of a month."[33]

Cherries are a good source of melatonin. Experts recommend eating a few or drinking a glass of tart cherry juice about an hour before bed.

The addition of the mineral calcium, which is found in dairy products, helps the brain efficiently use tryptophan to produce melatonin. Calcium is also a natural relaxant. This makes foods such as milk, yogurt, and cheese that contain both calcium and tryptophan top sleep-inducing foods. A bowl of cereal and milk; half of a turkey, cheese, or peanut butter sandwich on whole-grain bread with a glass of milk; a small bowl of yogurt with nuts; or whole-grain crackers and a glass of milk are all good sleep-inducing bedtime snacks.

Some experts also believe certain food intolerances contribute to narcolepsy. These include wheat, dairy, corn, and chocolate. An elimination diet may be helpful to some people. The website Healthline explained,

> *An elimination diet involves removing foods from your diet that you suspect your body can't tolerate well. The foods are later reintroduced, one at a time, while you look for symptoms that show a reaction.*
>
> *It only lasts 5–6 weeks … Once you have successfully identified a food your body can't tolerate well, you can remove it from your diet to prevent any uncomfortable symptoms in the future.*[34]

The Role of Exercise

Being physically active is another strategy that helps people sleep better. Exercise helps keep the body fit and healthy. It controls weight, which is especially helpful for people with sleep apnea, and reduces stress and anxiety. Exercise also tires the body, promoting a good night's sleep. A 2010 Northwestern University study looked at the effects of aerobic exercise—sustained physical activity such as running, walking, bicycling, dancing, and swimming—on a group of women with insomnia who were older than 55. Half the subjects exercised four times per week for either two 20-minute sessions or one 30- to 40-minute session. The other subjects acted as a control group: They did not exercise at all. Instead they participated in nonphysical activities such as museum lectures. After 16 weeks, the subjects who exercised showed a dramatic improvement in their sleep duration, sleep quality, and daytime energy levels, while the control group did not. The exercising group averaged an additional 75 minutes of sleep per night and a 33 percent reduction in nighttime arousals. The non-exercising group increased their amount of sleep time by only 12 minutes per night and showed no difference in their amount of nighttime arousals.

Despite such benefits, since exercise increases heart and respiration rate and raises body temperature, exercising too close to bedtime can actually make it harder to sleep. Sleep expert Dr. Michael Breus advised,

> *For the most sleep-enhancing exercise routine, get moving in the morning, and get outside in the sunlight. This early-in-the-day exertion and exposure to sunlight will strengthen your circadian rhythms, helping you to feel more alert during the day—and sleepier at night. If morning exercise doesn't fit in your schedule, find another time during the day that does. To avoid exercise interfering with winding down for sleep at night, schedule your workout no closer than 4 hours before bedtime.*[35]

Morning is the best time to exercise because it regulates the circadian clock, making people feel more awake during the day and sleepier at night.

Promoting Relaxation

Just as avoiding certain foods, drinks, and vigorous exercise right before bedtime helps improve sleep, so does establishing a consistent, soothing pre-bedtime routine 30 minutes to 1 hour before bedtime. Such a routine helps relax the body and signals the brain that it is time for sleep. For example, if individuals take a warm bath and massage body lotion onto their skin every night before going to bed, their brain eventually connects this routine with sleep and starts to wind down and prepare for bed. As Harvard University's Lawrence Epstein explained, "Our body craves routine and likes to know what's coming."[36]

Any activity that relaxes the body and mind can be part of this pre-bedtime routine. Soothing activities such as listening to soft music, hair brushing, reading a book, or writing in a journal are all activities that help people relax and prepare for sleep. Watching TV or playing a game may also feel relaxing, but these activities should be avoided because of the light from the screen.

For people who have difficulty shutting off their minds long enough to fall asleep, a mental exercise can help distract them from worrying or making plans. This can be something such as thinking of words that all start with the same letter, trying to remember every detail of their room with their eyes closed, mentally reciting song lyrics, or focusing "on the details of a particular object, such as its color, shape, size and what it's used for."[37]

Being aware of the body's reaction to light also helps people with sleep disorders sleep better. Exposure to light affects the body's natural circadian rhythm. Exposure to bright light at bedtime suppresses the production of melatonin, making it difficult to get to sleep, while limited exposure to light has the reverse effect. Brightly backlit devices, such as computers, tablets, and smartphones, are especially stimulating to the brain.

Digital clocks with a blue light display can also disrupt people's circadian rhythm; clocks with a red light display are less disruptive. However, the presence of any clock near the bed can cause problems for people with sleep disorders, who often find themselves checking the clock throughout the night instead of trying to relax. Therefore, people with sleep disorders may find it helpful to remove all bedroom clocks from view.

Creating the Best Environment

Other strategies involving light, such as keeping the bedroom dark, also help. Sleeping with the lights on can signal the brain that it is time to be awake. Even little bits of light can pass through the eyelids to the brain, reducing or stopping the production of melatonin. Sleep experts say it is best to turn off all the lights and draw the blinds and curtains. Special curtains called blackout curtains can be used by people such as night-shift workers, whose work schedules require them to sleep during the day, or by individuals whose bedrooms face brightly lit streets. Blackout curtains look like regular curtains, but they contain an insulating panel that blocks out almost all light. Alternatively, some sleepers wear an eye mask designed to help block out light.

Besides keeping the bedroom dark, taking other steps to turn the bedroom into a relaxing place helps promote sleep. Experts say that a temperature between 60 degrees and 68 degrees Fahrenheit (15 degrees and 20 degrees Celsius) makes it easiest to sleep. Temperatures too far below or above this range can cause restlessness. Scientists are unclear why room temperature is so important, but some, such as sleep expert Adam Tishman, say "this room temperature will help the body maintain a temperature slightly lower than 98.6 degrees,"[38] which is the natural sleeping body temperature for most people.

ASMR

Some people find that listening to people speak or hearing certain sounds, such as papers shuffling or beads clicking together, relaxes them and makes it easier for them to fall asleep. As a result, these videos have become increasingly popular on YouTube. They are posted under the label ASMR (autonomous sensory meridian response) because many people who enjoy these videos experience ASMR when they watch them. This is "a relaxing, often sedative sensation that begins on the scalp and moves down the body."[1] One ASMRtist—the name for people who make ASMR videos—described it as "the amazing chills you get when someone plays with your hair or traces your back with their fingertips."[2]

Many adults have seen episodes of *The Joy of Painting*, a daytime TV show featuring soft-spoken artist Bob Ross. Although the term ASMR was not coined until the early 2000s and Ross was not trying to create that response in his viewers, he was many people's first exposure to ASMR and is still one of the most popular YouTube searches for this topic. In recent years, many people have started creating their own ASMR channels, taking requests from viewers for things to include in future videos, and even gaining a bit of fame. As of 2016, there were about 5.2 million ASMR videos on YouTube, and interest has continued to grow since then. According to Think with Google, a website run by Google that analyzes search trends, "searches on Google tend to peak around 10:30 p.m., regardless of time zone, when people are winding down for the evening. 'ASMR sleep' is one of the top related terms."[3] Some therapists are even exploring the possibility of using ASMR to treat anxiety and insomnia.

Many people find Bob Ross's soft voice and the sounds of the paintbrushes on the canvas to be relaxing.

1. Allison Mooney and Jason Klein, "ASMR Videos Are the Biggest YouTube Trend You've Never Heard Of," Think with Google, September 2016. www.thinkwithgoogle.com/consumer-insights/asmr-videos-youtube-trend/.

2. Mooney and Klein, "ASMR Videos."

3.Mooney and Klein, "ASMR Videos."

The bedroom's air quality also has an effect on sleep quality, especially for people with allergies. Dust, mold, pet hair, and other allergens on the bed linens or in the bedroom can make it hard for some people to breathe. Instead of resting, these individuals are likely to spend the night sneezing and coughing. Using an air purifier with a high-efficiency particulate air (HEPA) filter helps because it removes allergens from the air. Additionally, since allergens tend to gather on soft surfaces, many people find that removing stuffed toys and decorative pillows from the bed helps, as does keeping pets off the bed.

Pets can interfere with sleep in other ways. If pets move around on the bed or make noise at night, they may awaken sleepers. Other noises can be a problem, too. To help eliminate disruptive noises, many sleepers use a white-noise machine—a device that produces a soothing background sound that masks other, more disturbing sounds. A fan or an air conditioner also helps mask sound. Some people use earplugs to block out sound or play a recording of a rainstorm, a waterfall, birdsong, or other natural noises.

A Comfortable Sleeping Space

A clean, comfortable, welcoming bed is another important element in creating a soothing sleep environment. In fact, 86 percent of the respondents to a National Sleep Foundation survey said clean sheets are an important element in getting a good night's sleep. Many people with sleep disorders find that frequently changing the sheets improves their sleep.

A comfortable, good-quality mattress and supportive pillows also promote sleep. A smooth, firm mattress provides the best support for a sleeper's back and neck. A sagging or lumpy mattress, on the other hand, can lead to nighttime arousals due to discomfort and cause individuals to wake up in the morning feeling stiff and sore. Many sleep experts suggest replacing mattresses every seven to ten years.

Keeping the bedroom clean and the bed made creates a more welcoming sleeping environment.

They also advise sleepers to replace their pillows often. Pillows support a sleeper's neck and head so these body parts do not feel overstretched or squeezed. The right pillow can make a significant difference in how well a person sleeps. For example, Hector, a middle-aged man with sleep problems, found that a new pillow specially designed for people with sleep troubles improved his sleep quality. He said, "I got a special pillow. It is wonderful. I have an old neck and shoulder injury and this pillow supports my head and shoulders, so I am not in pain. I love it. I no longer wake up during the night. I am sleeping a lot better."[39]

Certain other bed modifications are less common, but may be helpful to people with severe sleep disorders. For example, many people find that they sleep better when they are rocked to sleep. People who tend to fall asleep more easily in a hammock, a car, or a train may want to consider getting a rocking bed. Some companies make machines that replace a traditional box spring and rock the mattress from side to side. However, a rocking bed costs thousands of dollars, which may be too expensive for some people to afford.

Tracking Sleep Patterns

Many people are unaware that they are not getting good sleep until they start tracking things such as the time between when they go to bed and when they fall asleep, how many days in a row they went to bed later than they intended, and how many times they woke up during the night. New technology has made it easier than ever to track these patterns. In the past, people would have had no way to know things such as how much they moved around while they were sleeping or times when they woke up without knowing it. Now people can use wearable devices to help them see what is happening while they are sleeping.

One of the most popular sleep-tracking devices is FitBit. This device is worn on the wrist like a watch or bracelet. It connects to a phone app that displays health information in easy-to-read charts. Some FitBits include a silent alarm, which vibrates to wake the person instead of making a loud noise. Some experts believe this provides an easier transition between sleeping and waking. This can also be helpful for people who are deaf and cannot hear a traditional alarm. The sleep tracking app shows people how long it took them to fall asleep, how restless their sleep was (in other words, how often they moved around in bed), how many times they woke up during the night, how long they spent in REM sleep, and how this information compares to the recommended guidelines for a person of their age and sex. Seeing all of this information at a glance can make it much easier for someone to identify patterns and see what they may need to improve.

Although a FitBit can be helpful, the cheapest one with a sleep tracker is still more than $100, which may be too much for some people. A wearable device tends to provide the most accurate tracking, but there are some free apps people can use to help them with their sleep. Some of these include:

- **Sleep Cycle:** Available only for Apple's iPhone, Sleep Cycle works by detecting a person's movements with the same part of the phone that can detect a change in the phone's orientation from vertical to horizontal. People who use this app place it next to their pillow at night and the app records how often they move around in bed. Since people move less when they are in REM sleep, the app can use this information to determine the best time to have the wake-up alarm go off.
- **Sleep Better:** This app is similar to Sleep Cycle, but it can also detect when a person is snoring. Additionally, people can enter information about what they do when they are awake to help them see which activities correlate with the best night's sleep.
- **To Bed:** The user enters their age and what time they need to wake up, and the app sends them a notification at the time they should start preparing for bed.
- **Digipill:** This app provides meditation sessions it calls "pills," which are "prescribed" for things such as more restful sleep, improving mood, and reducing anxiety.

From replacing pillows to practicing good sleep hygiene, people with sleep disorders may have to make many lifestyle changes to improve their sleep. However, by doing so, they take control of their lives and improve their physical, mental, and emotional health.

CHAPTER FIVE

LOOKING FORWARD

There is still much more to learn about sleep, which is why research is ongoing. Scientists hope to understand why people need sleep, how to help them sleep better, and how to develop improved treatments—and possibly even cures—for common sleep disorders.

Studying Genetics

In a number of laboratory studies, scientists are trying to identify specific genes that regulate sleep. For example, in 2017, a team of international researchers discovered seven genes that put a person at risk for developing insomnia. Two of the genes have also been identified as risk factors in restless legs syndrome and another sleep-related movement disorder called periodic limb movement disorder. The study found that there is also a strong genetic correlation, or link, between insomnia and mental illnesses such as anxiety and depression. Anke Hammerschlag, one of the study's authors, said, "This is an interesting finding, because these characteristics tend to go hand in hand with insomnia. We now know that this is partly due to the shared genetic basis."[40]

Another study focused on identifying genes that regulate sleep. By studying mice whose genes had been chemically mutated, the researchers "identified the roles of two proteins in sleep/need regulation and in maintaining REM sleep periods."[41] One of the proteins made the mice sleep longer than normal, while the other made them have short, unstable REM sleep. Masashi Yanagisawa, the lead author of this study, said in 2016, "It is amazing that we know almost nothing about the simple question of what is 'sleepiness' physically in our brain. We will start from these genes and try to solve the great mystery."[42]

Effects on Other Brain Functions

Other researchers are taking a different approach. People with sleep disorders complain of mental fuzziness, memory problems, and difficulty learning. With this in mind, researchers are investigating the effect of sleep on the brain. One group of studies is focusing on the link between sleep, the formation and retention of memories, and learning.

Scientists believe that during N3 and REM sleep, the brain replays experiences from the day, which strengthens memory. The brain gathers information throughout the day, which is stored in a network of nerve cells that connect communication pathways in the brain. There is, however, only so much physical space in the skull for the network. Many scientists theorize that in order to create space for new learning, during sleep, the brain trims this neural network, discarding weaker connections and converting stronger connections into long-term memories. Two studies in 2009, conducted at Washington University in St. Louis, Missouri, and the University of Wisconsin at Madison, helped confirm this theory. In both studies, scientists examined the brains of fruit flies before and after sleep. Because they are easier to study than more complex animals, fruit flies have been used in studies for many years. Both studies found that after sleep, the volume of connections between nerve cells in the brain decreased in size and number. "If this didn't happen, theoretically, over time, the brain would reach capacity and be unable to learn or remember new things," explained Washington University researcher Paul Shaw. "After a night's sleep, the next morning the brain wakes up and is ready to go, ready to acquire new information."[43]

In 2011, another Washington University study established a link between sleep and the formation of long-term memories. In this study, the researchers altered a cluster of cells in the brains of fruit flies, which allowed the researchers to control the flies' sleep habits. To test whether sleep is connected to the formation of long-term memories, the researchers exposed male fruit flies to other male fruit flies that were genetically altered to smell like female fruit flies. After a few unsuccessful attempts to mate, the unaltered male flies learned to ignore the altered flies. Then, the researchers allowed some of the flies to sleep, while keeping others awake. The next day, the flies that slept did not attempt to mate with the altered flies. However, the flies that were deprived of sleep did. The researchers believe this means that the brain transforms new information into long-term memories during sleep and that without sleep, the brain is unable to convert short-term knowledge into long-term memories.

A 2011 Stanford University study found that the continuity of sleep was just as important in forming memories as the length of sleep. In this study, mice were exposed to new toys during the day. Then, the mice went to sleep. Half the mice were allowed to sleep normally, while the others were repeatedly awakened. Both groups slept for the same length of time. The next day, the mice were exposed to new

Fruit flies are popular subjects for genetic research because any changes made to their genes can be observed in a very short time.

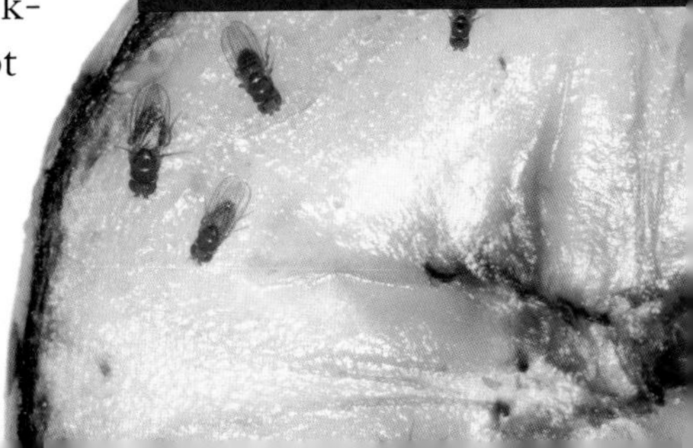

toys. The mice that slept continuously explored the new toys while ignoring the toys from the day before, while the mice whose sleep was disrupted explored the old toys as if they were unfamiliar.

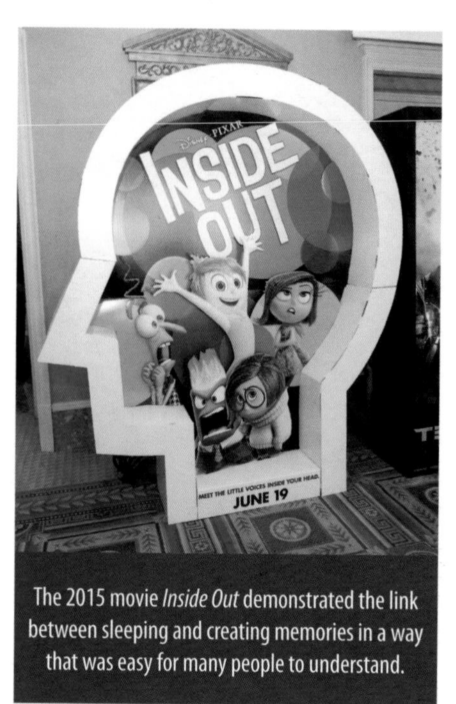

The 2015 movie *Inside Out* demonstrated the link between sleeping and creating memories in a way that was easy for many people to understand.

The Connection Between Dementia and Sleep

Reduced cognitive abilities and impairment of memory are also connected to dementia, a disorder that affects the brain. Research has already demonstrated that there may be a link between lack of sleep and the development of Alzheimer's disease—a type of dementia—due to the lack of opportunity for the brain to prune its neural networks. In addition, because lack of good-quality sleep affects the formation of memories and lack of oxygen is harmful to the brain, scientists at the University of California, San Francisco, investigated whether there was a link between the development of dementia and sleep apnea. The study began in 2006, when the researchers monitored the sleep of 298 physically and mentally healthy women with an average age of 82. Sleep monitoring showed that 105 of the subjects had sleep apnea. The women were also given tests that measured their memory and cognitive abilities. All the subjects were reexamined five years later. None of the subjects with sleep apnea had received treatment for the condition in those five years. After controlling for variables such as the presence of other

Dreaming and Problem-Solving

Sleep researchers are unsure why people dream. A 2010 study at Beth Israel Deaconess Medical Center in Boston, Massachusetts, suggests that dreaming helps learning. In this study, 99 adult subjects spent an hour trying to get through a virtual maze. Half the subjects then slept for 90 minutes, and half relaxed while awake. During the 90 minutes, the subjects were awakened or interrupted and asked to describe their dreams or thoughts. When the rest period was up, all the subjects tried to solve the maze again. The subjects who had stayed awake showed no improvement in their ability to solve the maze. The subjects who had slept but did not report any maze-related dreams improved slightly. The subjects who reported dreaming about the maze showed a significant improvement. The difference in their scores on the maze before and after dreaming was 10 times higher. Interestingly, the dreamers did not dream about solving the maze; the maze was simply part of their dream. For example, one subject dreamt about the music played during the task, while another dreamt about meeting people in the maze. The researchers theorize that dreams may be the brain's way of improving learning and creatively solving problems.

diseases, the use of certain medicines, and body weight that might impact the results, the researchers found that the subjects with sleep apnea were 85 percent more likely to have developed dementia or mild cognitive impairment than the other subjects.

Since the study monitored the subjects for only one night, the results require more research. A more recent study, published in 2017, contributed to the first study's findings. The 2017 study examined 208 people between the ages of 55 and 90 over the course of two years. Sleep tests found that more than half of the participants had untreated sleep apnea, and tests of their spinal fluid as well as brain scans found that the more apneas they had per hour, the higher their levels of a substance called amyloid beta. Past research has shown that high levels of amyloid beta in the brain contribute to the development of Alzheimer's disease. However, even more research is required to prove a definitive link; although the participants with more severe sleep apnea showed an increase in the amount of amyloid beta in their brains, they did not all show the decline in mental abilities associated with the disease. The researchers noted that this might have been partially because their participants were all highly educated, and past Alzheimer's research has shown that the more education a person has, the lower their risk of developing Alzheimer's in the future.

If further studies prove a definitive connection, it is likely that in the future, people with sleep apnea will be monitored for dementia symptoms. Additionally, because the link between sleep apnea and dementia shows how important it is that people with sleep apnea seek and stick with treatment, it should also lead to the development of newer sleep apnea treatments that more patients can tolerate.

How Sleep Affects Feelings

Other researchers are investigating whether sleep disorders impact emotions. Individuals with sleep disorders often complain that a lack of good-quality sleep causes them to feel cranky, agitated, and overemotional. A 2011 University of California, Berkeley, study looked at the connection between sleep problems and emotions. The results of the study suggest that emotional experiences are processed during REM sleep, so unpleasant experiences feel less painful and create less strong emotions upon waking.

In this study, researchers divided 35 adult subjects into 2 groups. Both groups were shown a series of pictures designed to produce powerful negative emotions. As they viewed the pictures, the subjects' brain activity was monitored with functional magnetic resonance imaging (fMRI). Both groups viewed the pictures twice with a 12-hour break between viewing. One group viewed the pictures in the morning and again in the evening, without sleeping in between.

Many people find that not getting enough sleep makes it harder for them to deal with negative emotions.

The other group viewed the pictures in the evening, then slept a full night—during which their sleep was monitored—before viewing the pictures again in the morning. The subjects who slept reported a decreased emotional reaction upon viewing the pictures the second time, and their fMRIs showed a significant decrease in activity in the region of the brain involved in emotions. The subjects who did not sleep between

Becoming a Sleep Specialist

Individuals trained in sleep science are currently in high demand in the job market and should continue to be in the future. Individuals interested in sleep can train to be doctors with a specialty in sleep disorders. This requires a four-year college degree followed by eight years of medical training. Training as a psychologist is another path to a career in sleep science. Psychologists must have a minimum of a four-year college degree. Scientists who specialize in sleep research also need a minimum of a four-year college degree. However, most scientists and psychologists go on to get advanced degrees.

There are not many jobs for nurses specifically devoted to sleep disorders. However, nurses interested in sleep can work for medical practices in related medical fields, including psychiatry, pulmonology (diseases of the respiratory system, including sleep apnea), and general medical practices. Nurses need either a two-year or a four-year degree in nursing, depending on what type of job they want to do. Sleep lab technicians or polysomnography technologists also need at least a two-year associate's degree from an accredited training program. Many community colleges offer certification in polysomnography.

viewings had no change in emotional reaction. The researchers noted that during REM sleep, the sleepers' brains suppressed the release of a chemical associated with stress and arousal, which led them to believe that a function of REM sleep is to soothe the brain after stressful experiences.

Continued studies into the relationship of REM sleep and emotions are likely, especially since this study had a very small sample size and further research is needed to see if the results apply to a larger population. "A greater understanding of this possible connection," Breus explained, "could have a profound effect on how we view, and treat, sleep problems and the secondary effects of sleeplessness."[44]

Another area of research is investigating whether there is a connection between sleep disorders and emotional and behavioral problems in children. A study at Albert Einstein College of Medicine in New York City studied 11,000 children for 6 years, ending in 2012. At various intervals, the subjects' parents answered a questionnaire about the children's sleep habits and another about the children's behavior. The behavior questionnaire assessed hyperactivity, inattentiveness, emotional issues, aggressiveness, and social skills. The researchers found the children with sleep-disordered breathing were at significantly greater risk of being hyperactive and having other emotional problems.

A 2015 study by researchers at the Norwegian University of Science and Technology found similar results. The team studied nearly 1,000 toddlers and discovered that "four-year-olds with sleep disorders have a higher risk of developing symptoms of psychiatric problems as six-year-olds, compared with children who sleep soundly."[45] The researchers also found that the reverse was true: Four-year-olds who showed psychiatric symptoms were more likely to develop a sleep disorder by the time they were six. This study showed how important it is to treat sleep disorders in children rather than waiting to see if they grow out of them.

A Controversial Treatment

Medical marijuana has become a popular treatment for many physical and mental health problems, including anxiety, chronic pain disorders, and insomnia. In 2018, marijuana was also approved in Minnesota to treat obstructive sleep apnea. However, opinions are divided in the medical community about whether this is a good idea. One 2002 study showed that marijuana improved sleep apnea in the test subjects by limiting "the effect of serotonin on cells in the inferior ganglion of the vagus nerve, which plays a role in breathing sensations."[1]

However, since the study only included 17 participants, it is unclear whether these results are typical. Other medical experts believe medical marijuana should not be used to treat sleep apnea. The American Academy of Sleep Medicine warned that due to the small sample size of the original study, there is no proof that marijuana is a safe or effective treatment for sleep apnea. Adding an extra dimension of uncertainty is the many ways people can use marijuana, including pills, oils, and creams. This means there is no set dose, which can cause unintended, occasionally dangerous side effects, such as daytime sleepiness.

1. "Sleep Apnea," Marijuana Doctors, accessed on August 1, 2018. www.marijuanadoctors.com/conditions/sleep-apnea/.

Food and Sleep

Other scientists are taking a completely different approach. They are investigating whether what individuals eat can relieve sleep disorders. Several studies, including a 2011 study at the University of Crete in Greece and a 2017 study at the University of Parma in Italy, have found that eating a Mediterranean-style diet could improve sleep quality and quantity. A Mediterranean diet is rich in fruit, vegetables, fish, whole grains, nuts, seeds, and healthy fats such as olive oil. It is considered to be very healthy and appears to help protect the body from a number of diseases.

Studies suggest that a Mediterranean diet may improve the quality and quantity of a person's sleep. However, it may not work for everyone.

In the 2011 study, the researchers divided 40 obese patients with sleep apnea into 2 groups. One group followed a low-calorie diet for 6 months. The other followed a Mediterranean diet. Both groups were encouraged to exercise for 30 minutes per day, and all the patients were given CPAP treatment. The patients' sleep was monitored at the start of the study and again 6 months later. The researchers found that the patients who followed the Mediterranean diet showed improvement during one stage of sleep, but not in overall improvement of the condition.

The 2017 study looked at 690 Italian school-aged children and found that the ones who ate a Mediterranean diet were not only more likely to get better quality sleep for longer, they also showed improvement in academic achievement and increased physical activity. Although it is unclear whether these last two are a direct result of the diet or simply of not being sleep-deprived, a Mediterranean diet may be worth investigating for someone with a sleep disorder. This and other new discoveries give hope to millions of people currently experiencing sleepless nights.

NOTES

Introduction: Understanding Sleep Disorders

1. "Sleep Disorders in Children," WebMD, January 20, 2017. www.webmd.com/children/sleep-disorders-children-symptoms-solutions#4.
2. David Dudley, "Quest for a Good Night's Sleep," *AARP the Magazine*, August/September 2016. www.aarp.org/health/conditions-treatments/info-2016/sleep-apnea-insomnia.html.
3. Quoted in Anita Bruzzese, "Going Nonstop All Day Can Thwart Productivity on the Job," *USA Today*, July 7, 2010. www.usatoday.com/money/jobcenter/workplace/bruzzese/2010-07-07-take-time-to-rest_N.htm.
4. "Why Is Sleep Important?," National Heart, Lung, and Blood Institute, accessed on July 16, 2018. www.nhlbi.nih.gov/node/4605.

Chapter One: How Sleep Works

5. Christopher French, "Why Did Sleep Evolve?," *Scientific American*, accessed on July 16, 2018. www.scientificamerican.com/article/why-did-sleep-evolve/.
6. Amanda MacMillan, "Why Dreaming May Be Important for Your Health," *TIME*, October 27, 2017. time.com/4970767/rem-sleep-dreams-health/.

7. MacMillan, "Why Dreaming May Be Important for Your Health."

8. "Sleep in Adolescents," Nationwide Children's Hospital, accessed on July 17, 2018. www.nationwidechildrens.org/specialties/sleep-disorder-center/sleep-in-adolescents.

9. "Say Goodbye to Sleep Debt," Sleep.org, accessed on July 17, 2018. sleep.org/articles/say-goodbye-sleep-debt/.

10. Quoted in Gayle Greene, *Insomniac*. Berkeley, CA: University of California Press, 2008, p. 108.

Chapter Two: The Effects of Sleep Disorders

11. Quoted in Greene, *Insomniac*, p. 122.

12. Aparna Ranjan, "Primary Insomnia," emedicinehealth, November 20, 2017. www.emedicinehealth.com/primary_insomnia/article_em.htm#what_is_the_outlook_for_a_person_with_primary_insomnia.

13. Quoted in "Share Your Sleep Story," Neurology and Sleep Medicine Consultants of Houston and the Houston Sleep Center. www.houstonsleepcenter.com/projectsleep.html.

14. "Patient Stories—Mike's Story," Talk About Sleep, July 12, 2013. www.talkaboutsleep.com/patient-stories-mikes-story/.

15. Jennifer Hines, "The 3 Types of Sleep Apnea Explained: Obstructive, Central, & Mixed," Alaska Sleep Clinic, July 13, 2018. www.alaskasleep.com/blog/types-of-sleep-apnea-explained-obstructive-central-mixed.

16. "Hypoventilation," American Sleep Association, September 2007. www.sleepassociation.org/sleep-disorders/more-sleep-disorders/hypoventilation/.
17. Kevin Phillips, "Sleep Bruxism (Teeth Grinding): Symptoms, Causes, & Treatment," Alaska Sleep Clinic, October 30, 2014. www.alaskasleep.com/blog/sleep-bruxism-teeth-grinding-symptoms-causes-treatment.
18. "How to Safely Wake a Sleepwalker," Sleep.org, accessed on July 18, 2018. sleep.org/articles/safely-wake-sleepwalker/.
19. "Sleep Eating Disorder—Overview & Facts," Sleep Education, accessed on July 18, 2018. sleepeducation.org/sleep-disorders-by-category/parasomnias/sleep-eating-disorder/overview-facts.
20. "About Narcolepsy," Narcolepsy Network, accessed on July 18, 2018. narcolepsynetwork.org/about-narcolepsy/.
21. Stephanie Handy and Tracy R. Nasca, "Life with Narcolepsy," Talk About Sleep, October 12, 2010. www.talkaboutsleep.com/sleep-disorders/2010/10/Life-With-Narcolepsy.htm.
22. Quoted in Ariel Neuman, "GHB's Path to Legitimacy: An Administrative and Legislative History of Xyrem," LEDA at Harvard Law School, April 2004. dash.harvard.edu/bitstream/handle/1/9795464/Neuman.html?sequence=2.
23. Handy and Nasca, "Life with Narcolepsy."

Chapter Three: Diagnosis and Treatment

24. Kevin Phillips, "What to Expect During an In-Lab Sleep Study," Alaska Sleep Clinic, August 27, 2014. www.alaskasleep.com/blog/what-to-expect-in-lab-sleep-study-polysomnography.

25. Gina Pera, "Wired, Tired, & Sleep Deprived," *ADDitude*, accessed on July 19, 2018. www.additudemag.com/wired-tired-sleep-deprived/.

26. Bill, "Patient Stories—Bill's Sleep Apnea Story," Talk About Sleep, July 12, 2013. www.talkaboutsleep.com/patient-stories-bills-sleep-apnea-story/.

27. Kiara Anthony, "5 Home Remedies for Sleep Apnea," Healthline, February 14, 2018. www.healthline.com/health/home-remedies-for-sleep-apnea.

Chapter Four: Living with a Sleep Disorder

28. "Sleep Hygiene: Healthy Hints to Help You Sleep," University of Maryland Medical Center, accessed on July 31, 2018. www.umms.org/midtown/health-services/sleep-disorders/patient-information/sleep-hygiene.

29. Russell Rosenberg, "How Alcohol Can Ruin Your Sleep," *Huffington Post*, August 1, 2011. www.huffingtonpost.com/russell-rosenberg-phd/alcohol-sleep_b_902578.html.

30. Lisa Turner, "Sleep Advice: 5 Foods to Help You Snooze," *Huffington Post*, January 25, 2010. www.huffingtonpost.com/lisa-turner/sleep-advice-5-foods-to-h_b_430606.html.

31. Quoted in Ella Brooks, "15 Sneaky Sleep Stealers," *Natural Health*, December 2011, p. 62.

32. Quoted in Jean Enersen, "Spicy Food at Bedtime Can Disrupt Sleep," King5.com, July 21, 2010. www.king5.com/health/Spicy-foods-may-be-keeping-you-up-at-night-98969739.html.

33. "Food and Drink that Promote a Good Night's Sleep," National Sleep Foundation, accessed on July 31, 2018. sleepfoundation.org/sleep-topics/food-and-drink-promote-good-nights-sleep.

34. Ryan Raman, "How to Do an Elimination Diet and Why," Healthline, July 2, 2017. www.healthline.com/nutrition/elimination-diet.

35. Michael Breus, "The Sleep-Weight Connection: Gender Matters," The Sleep Doctor, November 1, 2011. www.thesleepdoctor.com/2011/11/01/the-sleep-weight-connection-gender-matters/.

36. Quoted in Margarita Tartakovsky, "12 Ways to Shut Off Your Brain Before Bedtime," Psych Central. psychcentral.com/lib/2011/12-ways-to-shut-off-your-brain-before-bedtime/.

37. Tartakovsky, "12 Ways to Shut Off Your Brain Before Bedtime."

38. Audrey Noble, "It's Official: This Is the Best Temperature for Sleep, According to an Expert," *The Thirty*, January 22, 2018. thethirty.byrdie.com/best-temperature-for-sleep--5a6245ac15356.

39. Hector, interview by Barbara Sheen, July 18, 2012.

Chapter Five: Looking Forward

40. Quoted in Vrije Universiteit Amsterdam, "Insomnia Not Purely Psychological Condition: Insomnia Genes Found," ScienceDaily, June 12, 2017. www.sciencedaily.com/releases/2017/06/170612115358.htm.

41. Don Galeon and Sarah Marquart, "A New Genetic Discovery Could Help Us Regulate Sleep," Futurism, November 2, 2016. futurism.com/a-new-genetic-discovery-could-help-us-regulate-sleep/.

42. Quoted in Galeon and Marquart, "A New Genetic Discovery."

43. Quoted in Alice Park, "What Good Is Sleep? New Lessons from the Fruit Fly," *TIME*, April 2, 2009. www.time.com/time/health/article/0,8599,1889099,00.html.

44. Michael Breus, "Can Sleep Heal Painful Memories?," The Sleep Doctor, January 26, 2012. www.thesleepdoctor.com/2012/01/26/can-sleep-help-heal-painful-memories/.

45. Rick Nauert, "Childhood Sleep Disorders Linked to Long-Term Mental Problems," PsychCentral, May 7, 2015. psychcentral.com/news/2015/05/07/childhood-sleep-disorders-linked-to-long-term-mental-problems/84353.html.

GLOSSARY

bruxism: Teeth grinding.

cataplexy: Episodes of temporary paralysis connected to narcolepsy.

electroencephalograph (EEG): A machine that records brain waves.

genetic: Passed down from parent to child.

homeostasis: The body's maintenance of a balanced state.

hypocretin: A chemical released by the brain that helps regulate sleep.

melatonin: A chemical that helps regulate sleep and waking.

obesity: A condition marked by an abnormal amount of body fat, generally at least 20 percent above healthy weight.

polysomnograph: A machine that records sleep patterns.

sleep hygiene: Healthy sleep habits.

slow-wave sleep: Deep sleep characterized by slow brain waves, which occurs in N3 sleep.

ORGANIZATIONS TO CONTACT

American Sleep Apnea Association
641 S. Street NW, 3rd Floor
Washington, DC 20001
(888) 293-3650
asaa@sleepapnea.org
www.sleepapnea.org
This organization provides information about sleep apnea. Its website includes links to help sleep apnea sufferers connect with and support each other. Always ask a parent or guardian before participating in an online forum.

American Sleep Association
201 Rock Lititz Boulevard, Ste. 25C
Lititz, PA 17543
www.sleepassociation.org
The American Sleep Association provides information about sleep and sleep disorders.

Narcolepsy Network
P.O. Box 2178
Lynnwood, WA 98036
(888) 292-6522
narnet@narcolepsynetwork.org
www.narcolepsynetwork.org
The Narcolepsy Network is dedicated to helping people with narcolepsy. It offers information about the condition, support groups, and ongoing research.

National Sleep Foundation
1010 N. Glebe Road, Ste. 420
Arlington, VA 22201
(703) 243-1697
www.sleepfoundation.org
This foundation is dedicated to educating the public about the importance of sleep. It provides information on every aspect of sleep and sleep disorders, and its website includes a link to help people find a sleep professional near them.

FOR MORE INFORMATION

Books

Maharaja, Siva Ganesh. *Sleep Information for Teens, 2nd Edition*. Detroit, MI: Omnigraphics, Inc., 2018.
This book explains the biological process of sleep, why it is important, how to create good sleeping habits, and how sleeping disorders disrupt normal sleep.

Micco, Jamie A. *The Worry Workbook for Teens: Effective CBT Strategies to Break the Cycle of Chronic Worry and Anxiety*. Oakland, CA: New Harbinger Publications, Inc., 2017.
Many cases of insomnia are caused by long-term anxiety. This book helps teens calm their fears to help them sleep better.

Poole, Hilary W. *Sleep Disorders*. Broomall, PA: Mason Crest, 2016.
This book describes symptoms and treatments for common sleep disorders.

Schantz-Feld, Mali Rebecca. *Sleep Drugs*. New York, NY: Chelsea House, 2011.
This book looks at different sleep medications, how the drugs work, how they affect the brain and the body, and controversies surrounding them.

Websites

BrainPOP: Sleep
www.brainpop.com/science/ecologyandbehavior/sleep
Through movies, quizzes, and activities, this website explains the importance of sleep.

Sleep.org
sleep.org
This website, which is run by the National Sleep Foundation, provides answers to common questions about sleep, such as how sleep disorders affect health, why people dream, and how to get a better night's sleep.

Sleep Better
sleepbetter.org
This website includes information about sleep, including a quiz people can take to determine how well they sleep compared to others of their age and sex.

Talk About Sleep
www.talkaboutsleep.com
This website provides sleep information and resources, including information on sleep disorders, treatment, patients' stories, and forums to help people with sleep disorders connect with each other. Always ask a parent or guardian before participating in an online forum.

INDEX

A

B

C

D

E

F

G

H

I

J

K

L

M

N

O

P

R

S

T

U

V

W

Y

Z

PICTURE CREDITS

Cover (main) Tampo/Shutterstock.com; cover, pp. 1–6, 11, 15, 19, 22, 28, 33, 42, 45, 48, 52, 61, 64, 70, 75, 79, 81, 83, 85, 91–92, 94, 96, 103–104 (purple texture) wongwean/Shutterstock.com; back cover (texture) Evannovostro/Shutterstock.com; p. 7 gpointstudio/Shutterstock.com; p. 10 Photographee.eu/Shutterstock.com; p. 12 A. von Dueren/Shutterstock.com; p. 14 artellia/Shutterstock.com; p. 17 Yuganov Konstantin/Shutterstock.com; p. 20 Sharaf Maksumov/Shutterstock.com; p. 25 Ekaterina Markelova/Shutterstock.com; p. 26 Syda Productions/Shutterstock.com; p. 29 Sergey Mironov/Shutterstock.com; p. 32 robroxton/Shutterstock.com; p. 35 Yuriy Maksymiv/Shutterstock.com; p. 36 Anna Hoychuk/Shutterstock.com; p. 39 Africa Studio/Shutterstock.com; p. 40 EKramar/Shutterstock.com; p. 43 Barcroft Media/Getty Images; p. 46 Thomas Koehler/Photothek via Getty Images; p. 50 sbw18/Shutterstock.com; p. 52 Featureflash Photo Agency/Shutterstock.com; p. 53 michaelheim/Shutterstock.com; p. 55 Jb Reed/Bloomberg via Getty Images; p. 57 Jaren Jai Wicklund/Shutterstock.com; p. 62 Dima Aslanian/Shutterstock.com; p. 64 Stepanek Photography/Shutterstock.com; p. 65 KatyaPulina/Shutterstock.com; p. 67 Daxiao Productions/Shutterstock.com; p. 70 Acey Harper/The LIFE Images Collection/Getty Images; p. 72 Ursula Page/Shutterstock.com; p. 77 Sylvie Bouchard/Shutterstock.com; p. 78 Gabe Ginsberg/WireImage/Getty Images; p. 81 fizkes/Shutterstock.com; p. 84 Foxys Forest Manufacture/Shutterstock.com.

ABOUT THE AUTHOR

Simon Pierce grew up in Jamestown, New York. He later moved to New York City and completed his education at NYU. He now lives in Brooklyn with his partner and their son. He has written for various health and wellness publications over the past seven years. He and his family enjoy people-watching in the park or reading the names on cemetery headstones and inventing stories about them.